Traditional
SOUTH AFR
Cookery

HIPPOCRENE INTERNATIONAL COOKBOOK SERIES

Traditional WITHDRAWN
SOUTH AFRICAN
Cookery

Hildegonda Duckitt

HIPPOCRENE BOOKS
New York

Originally published by Maskew Miller Ltd., Cape Town.

Hippocrene paperback edition, 1996.

For information, address:
HIPPOCRENE BOOKS
171 Madison Avenue
New York, NY 10016

Library of Congress Cataloging-in-Publication Data

Duckitt, Hildegonda J.
    Traditional South Africa cookery / Hildagonda Duckitt.--
Hippocrene pbk. ed.
        p.   cm.
    Originally published: Standard Press.
    ISBN 0-7818-0490-6
    1. Cookery, SouthAfrican. 2. South Africa--social life and customs.
    I. Title.
TX725.S6D835   1996   96-21645
641.5968--dc20   CIP

Printed in the United States of America.

WEIGHTS AND MEASURES

1 gill	$= \frac{1}{2}$ cupful
1 pint	= 2 cupfuls
1 quart	= 4 cupfuls
1 lb. butter	= 2 cupfuls, packed tight.
1 lb. flour	= 4 cups sifted flour
1 lb. sugar	= 2 cups (granulated)
1 lb. powdered sugar	= $2\frac{1}{2}$ cups
1 oz. butter	= 2 level tablespoonfuls
1 oz. flour	= 4 level tablespoonfuls
1 teaspoonful liquid	= 60 drops

Tablespoon has sometimes been abbreviated to tbsp., and teaspoon to tsp.

All recipes should be read through, before measuring, mixing and cooking operations are started.

Traditional
South African
Cookery

HILDA DUCKITT'S RECIPES

A

ANCHOVIES ON TOAST

Toast some slices of bread before a sharp fire, butter well, and cut into pieces one and a half inches square, lay on each piece a slice of hard-boiled egg and a boned anchovy. Sprinkle over the whole chopped parsley, and stand it for 10 minutes in the oven. Serve on a hot dish with water-cress around.

APPLES
(A NICE WAY OF COOKING)

Wipe the apples, but do not peel them; core, quarter, and cut into slices. Have ready some syrup, made in the proportions of a pound of sugar to a pint of water, boiled quickly for 5 minutes—either moist or crystallized sugar. Throw the apples into the boiling syrup, boil rapidly for 1 hour, reckoned from its first boiling up—stir frequently. It should then be clear, and jellied, and stiff. The rapid boiling drives off the watery particles in steam. Cloves, cinnamon, or lemon-peel may be added to taste.

APPLE CAKE
(This being a pudding is not put with other cakes. MRS. STRACHEY'S)

Ingredients:

1½ lb. apples, peeled and cored, cut in quarters	1 lb. white sugar
	½ pint of water

Boil the syrup, then add the apples, let them boil till quite soft and in a pulp. Add the juice and rind of a lemon grated. To be done over a quick fire—half an hour. Put into a mould, serve cold, with custard or cream.

APPLE CHARLOTTE
(MY OWN)

Ingredients:

1 doz. apples	1 tbsp. of butter
½ lb. of sugar	A few cloves or cinnamon
1d. loaf of white bread, crumbled very fine	A wineglass of wine

Butter a pie-dish, place in it alternately a layer of bread-crumbs (dotted with butter), slightly sprinkled with spice, a layer of sugar, and then one of apples. Fill the dish, taking care to have a layer of crumbs at the top, pour over it a glass of wine. Bake a nice brown; will take 1½ hours. (I generally have a tin cover over the dish for the first half-hour to steam it a little.) Turn out of the dish, and serve hot.

SWISS APPLE CHARLOTTE

Ingredients:

10 or 12 apples	¼ lb. moist sugar
Bread and butter	2 lemons

Take the crust from a stale loaf, and cut slices of bread and butter from the crumb. Butter the inside of a pie-dish and line it with the bread and butter, then add a layer of apples, pared, cored and cut in slices; strew over them lemon-peel cut very fine, and sugar; continue adding apples, lemon-peel and sugar until the dish is full. Squeeze over the whole the juice of 2 lemons, and cover the dish with the bread-crusts and peel of the apples to prevent burning. Bake an hour in a quick oven; when done remove the crusts and peels, turn out in a dish carefully. *Serve with a thin custard.* (*See* Custard.)

APPLE HEDGEHOG, OR ICED APPLES

Ingredients:

3 doz. good cooking apples	The rind of a lemon minced very
¼ lb. sugar	fine
A few sweet almonds	The whites of 2 eggs
	3 tbsps. pounded sugar

Peel and core a dozen of the apples without dividing, then stew in a tin-lined saucepan with half-pound of sugar and pint of water, and when tender lift them carefully on a dish. Have ready the remainder of the apples, cored and sliced, put them into the same syrup with the lemon-peel, and boil gently till reduced to a pulp; keep stirring to prevent burning. Cover the bottom of a dish with some of this apple marmalade, then a layer of the whole apples, and fill up the cavities with the marmalade, then another layer, and so on, forming the whole in a raised oval shape. Whip the whites of the eggs to a stiff froth, mix with the pounded sugar, and cover the apples very smoothly all over with the icing. Blanch and cut some almonds into 4 or 5 strips, stick these strips in upright at equal distances over the icing like the spines of a hedgehog, and place the dish in a slow oven for a few minutes before serving.

APPLE SHAPE

Ingredients:

1 lb. apples	¾ oz. gelatine
1 lb. sugar	A little lemon or clove seasoning

Add a teacup of water to the sugar, boil for 5 minutes. Cut the apples neatly into quarters, core them and stew in the syrup till clear. Take out the apples and put them neatly in a buttered mould. Soak the gelatine, add to the syrup, let it boil a little, and when slightly cooled pour into the mould. Turn out when cold, serve with custard or whipped cream. *Very good indeed.*

APPLE SNOW (D)
(MISS BREDA'S)

Ingredients:

6 large apples	2 eggs
¼ packet gelatine	3 oz. sugar
Lemon	

Cut up and reduce the apples to a pulp by boiling, pass through a strainer or sieve, put back into the saucepan with the gelatine soaked in a wineglass of water, pour into a basin to cool. Whisk the whites of the eggs to a stiff froth, sweeten with the sugar, and add the juice of the lemon; whisk the whole till it begins to set. Pile it high on a glass dish and arrange small pieces of red currant or quince jelly round it. Make a custard of the yolks to serve with the apple snow.

STEWED APPLES AND CUSTARD

Ingredients:

8 good-sized apples	The rind of half a lemon
4 cloves	½ pint custard (*see* Custard)
¾ pint water	1 doz. almonds
½ lb. sugar	

Pare and core the apples, but do not divide them, and if possible leave on the stalks; boil the sugar and water for 10 minutes, then put into the syrup with the lemon-rind and cloves, and simmer gently till tender. *Do not let them break.* Reduce the syrup by boiling quickly, let it cool a little, then pour over the apples. Have ready half a pint of thick custard, pour *round* the apples. Lastly, stick into the apples one dozen almonds, blanched and cut into strips. Takes 20 to 30 minutes to stew. This quantity will fill a large dish.

APRICOTS, DRIED AND SALTED
(COMMONLY CALLED MEBOS)

Take soft ripe apricots, lay them in salt water (about 2 ounces of salt to a quart bottle) for a few hours. Then lay them on a mat to dry in the sun; the next day press them between the hands to flatten, and to let the stones come out. The next day repeat the process. At the Cape it generally dries and becomes Mebos in 3 or 4 days in the sun, but if the weather should be damp, they might be dried in heated rooms, or a cool oven. To crystallize the Mebos, lay them in lime water (*see* Lime Water) for 5 minutes, till they feel nice and tender, take out, and wipe dry on a soft cloth, and rub coarse crystallized white sugar well into each; take 1½ lb. of white sugar to 1 lb. of Mebos. Pack closely with lots of sugar in between, in jars that will cork well. *A very nice sweetmeat, and said to be a remedy for sea-sickness.*

9

APRICOTS.—*See also* Peaches in Brandy, Marmalade (Apricot), and Pudding (Apricot Cream).

ASPIC.—*See* Jelly.

B

BEEF.—*See* Brine and Round of Beef (Spiced).

BEEF À LA MODE

Ingredients:

10 lb. round of beef (the bone taken out)
2 tsps. of salt
2 tsps. of pepper
1 oz. fine saltpetre

A tsp. of ginger, mace, allspice, cloves, and coriander seeds (*altogether*)
A tbsp. of vinegar
Strips of fat bacon for larding
Tbsp. of brown sugar

Hang the beef till quite tender. The day before cooking, spread over it a mixture of the above spices, moistened with vinegar. The next day fill the hole where the bone was taken out with a highly seasoned stuffing of bread-crumbs, suet, parsley, thyme, and a few shreds of onion; skewer, and roll a good shape; lard with strips of fat bacon. Put it on a small *tripod* on a baking-dish into the oven. Half an hour before the meat is done, pour over it half a tumbler of red wine into which a spoonful of flour has been stirred.

This is excellent cold, and takes 4 or 5 hours to cook.

ANOTHER RECIPE FOR BEEF À LA MODE
(A NICE WAY OF STEWING BEEF. AN OLD CONSTANTIA RECIPE)

Ingredients:

6 lb. or 8 lb. of round of beef
8 large onions
8 or 10 cloves, allspice, pepper

½ tumbler of wine and vinegar or tomato sauce
A few bay leaves and carrots

Slightly brown the onions in butter or dripping. Skewer the meat if a round; but it may be any other part—ribs, etc. Lay the onions on the top. Put it in a Dutch baking-pot, with the spices, vinegar, etc., and let all simmer for 2 hours, basting occasionally. It should be a nice brown. If it should want a little gravy, add some stock and half a cup of tomato sauce.

BEEF FRITTERS.—*See* Fritters.

BEEF OLIVES
(Mrs. Jackson's)

Cut rumpsteaks into strips 3 or 4 inches long, quarter of an inch thick. Sprinkle with fine bread-crumbs, pepper, salt, thyme; roll up, tie with a thread. Fry some onions in butter or fat; add to this one pint of water and some bay leaves. Stew the beef gently for an hour. Just before serving, remove the thread and dredge the gravy with some brown flour to thicken.

BEEF — SPICED
(Mrs. Cloete's)

Ingredients:

15 lb. centre ribs of beef	2 oz. cloves
1½ lb. salt	2 oz. allspice
¼ lb. sugar	2 doz. coriander seeds
2 oz. saltpetre	

Bruise these spices. Moisten all the ingredients with a cup of vinegar, rub well into the beef, let it remain 5 or 6 days in the mixture. Boil gently for 5 hours. Take care to let the water boil when you put in the meat.

BEEFSTEAK — BROILED

Take a nice tender steak, about 1½ or 2 inches thick and beat with a wooden kitchen mallet, to make it tender. Heat the gridiron on wood coals, and rub the bars with fat or butter. Sprinkle the steak with pepper and salt; turn frequently. Takes about 10 minutes. Serve immediately it is done—with a sauce made with some ketchup, or tomato sauce, and a lump of butter—*very hot.*

BEEFSTEAK PIE (D)

The meat for this pie, if for 3 or 4 people, is 1 lb. Australian steak. I find that washing this meat with warm water, and then wiping quickly, thaws it nicely. Cut the steak in pieces 4 inches square and hammer it well, or beat with the blunt side of a kitchen knife, then lay it for *half an hour in some milk*—this seems to give back to the meat all the flavour it has lost, and makes it very tender. Roll the pieces of meat in flour, pepper and salt mixed, and a few slices of onion. Stew it in the pie-dish on the stove for a quarter of an hour—now put over the crust (*see* Crust for Beefsteak pie or German tart), and bake for an hour on the floor of the oven.

BEEFSTEAK — STEWED

Ingredients:

2 lb. of steak	Tomato sauce
1 oz. butter	Pepper, salt
1 onion	A tsp. of brown flour

Fry the steak quickly in butter, then put in a stewpan with half a pint of water, 1 onion, and all the above ingredients—a little cayenne. Cover the pan close, having warmed the water before adding the meat (and the onion to be browned also before adding). Stew all gently for an hour. Thicken the gravy with butter rolled in flour. *Enough for 6 people.*

BILTONG
(An old Cape way of curing and drying meat)

Take about 6 or 8 pounds of beef, cut out in a long tongue-shape, out of the hind leg of an ox, from the thigh-bone down to the knee-joint. There are two such pieces in each leg, being quite encased in a fleecy skin. Take this meat, which is quite free from sinew or fat, first rub it with a little salt, and an hour after rub in well half a pound of salt, half a pound of brown sugar, and an ounce of saltpetre. Leave for three days, rubbing and turning every day; then put it in a press for a night. Have it dried in the wind, and then hung in the chimney till it is dry and pretty firm. When eaten it is to be cut into *very* thin slices—or rasped. Invalids like this way best; in fact, with bread and butter, Biltong is most appetising and nourishing; and, on board ship, people suffering from *Mal de Mer* have relished this when no other delicacy would tempt them to eat.

BISCUITS.—*See* Tea Cakes.

BLANCMANGE

Ingredients:

1 oz. gelatine	Juice of 3 lemons
Breakfast-cup of milk or cream	3 good tbsps. sugar
Yolks of 3 eggs	3 cups of milk

Soak the gelatine in a cup of milk. Boil the rest of the milk; stir in the yolks carefully, then the gelatine, lemon, sugar. Whisk the whites; stir into the mixture after it has boiled *once*. Remove from the fire; put in a buttered mould. Make overnight. *Enough for 4 or 5.*

BLATJANG
(Malay. Appetising condiment)

Ingredients:

A handful of red chillies, ground fine	2 onions, baked in oven and mashed very finely in a mortar.
40 sweet almonds	2 tiny pieces of garlic
1 tbsp. Apricot jam	2 lemon or bay leaves
A tsp. salt	2 tbsps. of lemon juice

Mix all well together. This condiment should be made fresh as required.

BLATJANG (D)

Soak 1 lb. dried apricots overnight in vinegar. Remove seeds from ¼ lb. fresh red chillies and pass them twice through the mincing-machine. Remove outer skins of 12 large flat white onions, bake them in the oven in an enamelled dish, and also mince. Now mash or mince the apricots. Add to these ingredients ½ lb. brown sugar, ¼ lb. salt, 2 tablespoonfuls coriander seeds, 1 large garlic, ½ lb. Valentia almonds, minced, 2 bottles of vinegar (Crosse and Blackwell's, or very good Cape vinegar). Boil all the ingredients together till nice and clear, *stirring all the time*, and when done put in small jars and cork well. Will keep a year. ½ lb. cayenne pepper may be used instead of chillies, but the blatjang will not have such a nice red colour.

BLOATER TOAST

Ingredients:

1 tsp. bloater paste	1 oz. of butter
1 tsp. anchovy sauce	A little cayenne
1 tbsp. of cream or milk	

Put these ingredients in a small jam-pot. Place the pot in a saucepan of boiling water; stir till it becomes a thick custard. Spread on buttered toast—crust cut off. *Sufficient for 2.*

BOBOTIE

(A DELICATE INDIAN MINCED CURRY. MALAY OR INDIAN. MY MOTHER'S)

Ingredients:

3 lb. of meat	2 tbsps of curry-powder
2 onions	A dessertsp. of sugar
A large slice of white bread	Juice of a lemon, or 2 tbsps. vinegar
1 cup of milk	6 or 8 almonds
2 eggs	Lump of butter

Mince the meat, soak the bread in milk, and squeeze out dry. Fry the onions in a tablespoonful of butter (dripping will do). Mix all the ingredients—curry-powder, sugar, salt, vinegar, etc., etc.—with the fried onion. Now mix all the meat and soaked bread. Mix 1 egg with the mixture, whisk the other with some milk, and pour over the whole, after being put into a buttered pie-dish or into little cups (the old Indian way), with a lemon or bay leaf stuck into each little cup. Put them in the oven to bake, and send to table in the cups or pie-dish. Serve with rice. (This dish is equally good made of cold mutton.)

1 oz. of Tamarinds soaked in half a pint of boiling water, then strained, and the juice used for Bobotie, Sasaties, and Curries instead of vinegar, gives a very pleasant acid flavour.

13

BRAWN

Ingredients:

2 calves' feet or 12 trotters
¼ bottle of vinegar
12 allspice
About 24 peppercorns
A tbsp. coriander seeds

The spices to be tied up in a muslin
   bag.
3 or 4 bay leaves
3 red chillies

Boil the sheep's feet quite tender, and when cold and firmly jellied remove the fat and bones. Boil with the spices and vinegar for an hour. Little pieces of sheep's tongue may be cut up in it. Pour into moulds, garnished with eggs, lemon, and parsley.

BRAWN—SHEEP'S TROTTERS (D)

Take 6 sheep's trotters, well cleaned and washed, first in warm water to which a pinch of washing soda has been added, and then again in cold water. Joint the trotters, cut up, and boil in an enamelled saucepan, with a good deal of water, till quite tender, so that the bones can be removed, and then after extracting the bones, set them to cool.

Skim off the oil to keep (this when clarified is equal to Lucca oil), and put the following ingredients—1 blade of mace, 1 dessertspoonful of salt, 25 peppercorns, a dessertspoonful of coriander seeds, 4 bay leaves—into a small muslin bag, and let them boil up with the jelly; add half a tumbler of vinegar. Let all boil together. Have ready some porcelain moulds dipped in water, or moistened with vinegar. Garnish the moulds with fresh red chillies cut up, a few slices of lemon, parsley, and even a slice or two of beet-root, and hard-boiled eggs. Remains of cold tongue, or little sheep's tongues, will improve the brawn. Take out the muslin bag and pour the brawn into the moulds. Some of the hard-boiled egg, and other garnishings, can be interspersed by adding pieces when you have poured a little brawn in, and then adding more brawn over, and so on, so that the egg is imbedded in the brawn. (Two calves' feet can also be cooked this way equally well.)

BREAKFAST DISHES.—*See* Brawn, Croquettes, Chicken (Scalloped), Eggs (Curried), Eggs (Poached), Eggs (Scratched), Fried Bread, Fish Fritters (Beef, etc.), Ham Toast, Herrings, Kedgeree, Kidneys, Mushrooms, Mutton Chops, Omelettes, Oysters (Scalloped), Porridge, Ragout, Rissoles, Rolls, Sausages, Scones, Cheese dish (another Risotto), Sheep's Brains, Polonies, Tea Cakes (Welsh Titiens), Herrings, Brawn, Fish.

BREAD SAUCE.—*See* Sauce.

BREAD — BROWN
(Our old Groote Post Recipe. Cape)

Take about 6 lb. of meal, pour into it 3 cups of home-made yeast (*see* Yeast), and as much tepid water as will make it the consistency of dough. Knead it well for a quarter of an hour, till your hand comes clean out of the dough. Set it to rise in the pan in which you have mixed it, and cover it up well. Put in the *warmest corner* of the kitchen. It will be ready for making into loaves in 2 hours, and will then have a rather disagreeable odour and feel quite spongy. 6 lb. of meal will just fill an ordinary baking pan for a moderate-sized stove oven. Keep the stove well heated, and when it has been in the oven for an hour turn the baking round. Bread made in this way is generally very sweet and wholesome. (*See* Loaf.)

BREAD—YEAST FOR HOME-MADE (D)

Ingredients:

1 teacupful of hops	(N.B.—No salt is to be added to
1 lb. potatoes	the yeast, but to the flour for
2 quarts water	the dough.)

Boil the hops and potatoes in the water for an hour, let it cool and strain. Then add 4 tablespoonfuls of flour and 4 of sugar and mix well. Put in any well-corked fruit-jar; Mason or Hazel jar will do. All air is to be excluded for 24 hours, when the yeast will be fit for use. Keep it in a cool place.

BREAD (D)

Use half a teacup of above yeast for 4 lb. flour, and screw up your jar again, it will keep for several bakings. The flour should be mixed with hot water and kneaded till no dough sticks to the hand; let it rise for 2 or 3 hours, keeping the dough warm, and bake in a good warm oven. It is best to arrange for the bread to be baked while the dinner is cooking, which is, of course, a great saving.

BREAD — PLUM i.e. CURRANT (D)

Ingredients:

1 lb. flour	2 tsps. baking-powder
¼ lb. currants	Milk
6 oz. sugar	

Mix with milk and bake in a flat tin, in a hot oven.

BREAD—RAISIN (D)
(MISS CARTWRIGHT'S)

Ingredients:

2 lb. flour
¾ lb. sugar
¼ lb. raisins
Ground cinnamon
Grated nutmeg

Spoonful crushed aniseed
1 tbsp. baking-powder
3 oz. butter (or 2 oz. butter and 1 oz. ox-marrow)

Mix with milk, 2 or 3 eggs could be added. Roll into 2 good loaves and bake in a quick oven for an hour.

BREDIE — A FAVOURITE CAPE STEW
(MALAY)

Take 2 lb. of thick rib of mutton, or in ordering 4 lb. of cutlet meat, take all that is rejected after carefully cutting and paring the cutlets. Take this meat, carefully cut in small pieces, put into a stewing-pot with 2 onions cut small. Let the meat and onion fry to a nice brown —*don't* burn. A rather quick fire is required for browning onions. Take one dozen or more large tomatoes cut in slices or pass through a mincing machine. If the tomatoes are not quite ripe add a teaspoonful of sugar, salt, a small piece of red chilli; let the tomato and meat stew gently; if watery, remove the lid of pot till there is a thick gravy. Bredies are not to be made in *deep* saucepans, but in flat pots, as they would be too watery in the former. Meat can be done with any vegetable in this way. Cauliflower, potato, vegetable marrow, make good Bredie. (*See* Tomato Bredie).

BOONTJIEBREDIE — DRY BEAN STEW
(CAPE OR MALAY)

Take 1 lb. of ribs of mutton, the fat part; set on the fire with a small onion cut in rings to brown slightly; then add a pint of water, about 2 or 3 cups of dry beans. If the beans are old, parboil them for ½ hour; strain through a colander and add to the meat. Stew till nice and tender for an hour or two. Add a red chilli, cut up. This is a favourite Cape Dish. Any kind of dry bean done in this way is very nice.

6 or 8 quinces, peeled, cored, and sliced, make a very good Bredie. If the quinces are acid and hard, parboil them and add a little sugar.

Parsnips are very good stewed with the meat.

BRINE FOR TONGUE OR BEEF

Ingredients:

6 tbsps. of salt
1 tbsp. of saltpetre.
2 tbsps. of brown sugar

2 cups of water
A few bay leaves

Pour over tongue or lump of beef after it has been rough-salted.

BROODKLUITJIES — BREAD DUMPLINGS
(AN OLD-FASHIONED DUTCH RECIPE)

Soak 3 large slices of stale white bread in broth till quite soft, squeeze out well, stir into a saucepan with a spoonful of butter. When well mixed, let it cool, add salt, pepper, nutmeg, finely-chopped parsley; beat up 2 eggs into the mixture. Now make into little round balls and roll in flour, add this to a stewed chicken or in good clear soup; it has only to boil up once, and will be found light and nourishing.

BUNS.—*See* Mosbolletjies.

BUTTER-SCOTCH

Ingredients:

¼ lb. butter
1 lb. sugar

¼ a tea-cup of water

Boil till quite thick. Pour on to a buttered dish, and cut into squares.

C

CABBAGE.—*See* Vegetable Savoury, and Pickled Cabbage (Atjaar).

CALF'S HEAD—MOCK TURTLE RAGOUT (D)
(MRS. CARL BECKER'S)

Boil a nicely-cleaned calf's head in water, add to it some salt, 20 peppercorns, a few bay leaves, and a white onion. Boil for 3 hours, or until quite tender, and see that the bones can be easily removed. Cut the meat into square pieces. Now make a sauce in a frying-pan by taking 2 oz. butter, let the butter get brown in the pan, then add a tablespoon of flour and stir it about till it is smooth; add to this a cupful of the stock in which the meat was boiled, and also a wineglass of sherry, and some cayenne pepper. Let this gravy get boiling hot, then put the squares in it before serving. This dish may be served with mushrooms or truffles and so done makes a nice entrée.

17

CAKE — ALMOND
(Mrs. Versfeld's old Dutch)

Ingredients:

1 lb. Almonds, blanched and
    pounded with rose-water
1 oz. bitter almonds
1 lb. loaf sugar (sifted)

10 eggs
5 tbsps. finest pounded biscuit
(500 almonds go to a lb.)

Blanch and pound the almonds, beat up the yolks of the eggs, mix with the sugar; then add alternately the whites and almonds, then the biscuit. Bake in a well-buttered mould for an hour and a half in a moderate oven, with a buttered paper over the mould. *Very good.*

CAKE — ALMOND, No. 1 (D)
(Miss Breda's)

Ingredients:

½ lb. sweet almonds and 15 bitter
    almonds, all blanched and well
    minced
¼ lb. flour

½ lb. finely-sifted sugar
6 eggs, of which you beat the whites
    and yolks separately

Mix in the following order: First the yolks with the sugar, then add the almonds, lastly the whites and flour alternately. Butter the mould well and dust with fine flour, or dried bread-crumbs finely pounded, put buttered paper over the top. Bake the cake 1 hour in a slow oven as you do sponge-cake.

CAKE — ALMOND, No. 2 (D)

Ingredients:

3 cups flour
2 cups sugar
2 well-beaten eggs
2 tbsps. butter
1 cup milk

30 sweet almonds
10 drops of essence of almonds
½ tsp. soda
1 tsp. cream of tartar

Mix and bake ingredients same as Almond Cake No. 1.

CAKE — BERG RIVER
(Mrs. Melck's)

Ingredients:

7 eggs
Their weight in sugar
The weight of 3 eggs in flour
25 sweet almonds

10 bitter almonds
Some citron preserve
1 lemon

Whisk the whites to a froth the whites and sugar to be mixed first, then the yolks and other ingredients. Bake in buttered mould for 1 hour. *Good.*

CAKE — BIRTHDAY
(MRS. ANDREW'S)

Ingredients:

1 lb. of finest flour
¾ lb. sugar
¾ lb. butter
1 lb. currants
¼ lb. almonds blanched and cut small

½ lb. chopped raisins
7 eggs
¼ lb. candied preserve
1 glass brandy
A few cloves; cinnamon, nutmeg, ginger

Beat the butter to a cream, mix with the sugar, then eggs, yolks first, then whites, then flour, currants, etc.; mix all very well. Bake in well-buttered mould for 2 hours, with buttered paper over, in moderate oven.

CAKE — BUTTERMILK
(A CHEAP, HOMELY CAKE)

Ingredients:

5 cups flour
2 cups sugar
1 cup currants
1 tbsp. butter
1 bottle buttermilk

2 tbsps. cinnamon
Some "Nartje" (tangerine Orange) peel
Vanilla Essence may be used instead
2 tsps. carbonate of soda

Mix the butter and sugar; then mix with the flour the spices, soda and currants. Stir in alternately a little flour and buttermilk. Have ready buttered moulds. Bake in a moderately quick oven.

CAKE — CHOCOLATE

Ingredients:

Whites of 7 eggs
1 lb. sugar

¼ lb. grated chocolate

First roll the chocolate and sugar together, whisk the whites stiffly mix with sugar and chocolate. Drop on a well-buttered paper. Let it stand for an hour to dry before putting into the oven which is not very warm. Bake about 10 minutes. When quite cold remove from the paper.

CAKE — COCOANUT
(MRS. REID OF SWELLENDAM'S)

Ingredients:

1 large or 2 small cocoanuts
1 lb. loaf sugar
6 eggs

½ lb. butter
¾ lb. flour

Beat the butter to a cream with the sugar; add the yolks well beaten, then the whites whisked to a froth, then the flour. When ready for the oven stir in the cocoanut. Bake for one hour and a half with paper over the mould.

19

CAKE — DUTCH
(Mrs. Faure's)

Ingredients:

1 lb. flour	1 glass of milk
1 lb. sugar	1 tsp. of soda
½ lb. butter	2 tsps. of cream of tartar
4 eggs	Any flavouring you like; makes excellent cake without any.

Stir butter to a cream, mix with eggs well beaten, flour, and milk, lastly the soda and cream of tartar. Bake one hour and a half in a moderate oven.

CAKE — GENOA

Ingredients:

¼ lb. butter	4 well-beaten eggs
8 oz. castor sugar	2 oz. almonds blanched
¼ lb. sultana raisins	Grated rind of a lemon
2 oz. mixed peel	2 tsps. of baking-powder
10 oz. flour	

Stir the butter till it is like cream; mix with it by degrees the eight ounces of sugar, four eggs, yolks and whites beaten separately; then add the ten ounces of flour, half a pound of raisins. Have ready the two ounces of almonds blanched, and lastly the grated rind of one lemon, and two teaspoons of baking powder, and the mixed candied peel. Butter the tin and line it with buttered paper, the paper to project half an inch above the rim of the tin. Pour in the mixture, and bake in a cool oven for an hour and a half. Sprinkle a few cut-up almonds over the top. *Very good.*

CAKE — GEORGINA'S
(AUNT FANNY'S)

Ingredients:

12 eggs and their weight in flour	20 sweet and 20 bitter almonds
1 lb. loaf sugar	blanched and sliced
¼ lb. butter	A little citron preserve
1 cup of currants	

Stir the butter to a cream, mix with loaf sugar; whisk whites and yolks separately, mix yolks with sugar and butter, then alternately add flour and whites, and lastly the currants. Bake with paper over the buttered mould for one and a half hours. Remove the paper and leave for another quarter of an hour. *Very good.*

CAKE — GERMAN
(Mrs. van der Riet's)

Ingredients:

1 lb. flour
1 lb. white sugar
¼ lb. butter
½ bottle of milk
¼ tsp. of soda

4 eggs
50 almonds
1 tea-cup of crystallized sugar and cinnamon

Mix in the ordinary way, and when ready for the oven have ready a flat baking-tin, or several tin plates buttered. Pour this dough into it, and spread thinly over the surface. Have ready the fifty almonds, roughly pounded, with cup of crystallized sugar and tablespoon of cinnamon; sprinkle thickly over the cake. Bake in moderately quick oven for twenty minutes. Cut into squares or shapes.

CAKE — GOLDEN

Ingredients:

½ lb. of butter
1½ lb. white sugar
3 cups of flour
½ cup of milk
Yolks of 6 eggs

White of 1 egg
Tsp. of cream of tartar
½ tsp. of soda
Essence of almonds, 20 drops

Stir the butter to a cream, mix with sugar; whisk the eggs, add to the sugar and butter, then add flour, lastly the soda and cream of tartar. Put into a buttered mould dusted with fine biscuit. Bake in a moderate oven for one and a half hours.

CAKES — KAIINGS
(Colonial, Miss Lizzie Cloete's)

Ingredients:

2 lb. flour
1½ lb. very dark brown sugar
2 cups kaiings (that is the dry scraps of any minced sheep tail fat or suet after it has been fried, and the boiling fat drained from it).

2 tbsps. of ground ginger
2 tbsps. of cinnamon
1 tbsp. baking powder, or 2 tsps. of soda and cream of tartar

Mix all the ingredients with flour and sugar dry, then moisten with lukewarm water into a stiff dough; roll out then and cut into small cakes. Bake in flat tins in a quick oven. Another recipe omits the cinnamon from ingredients, but adds a cup of buttermilk or thick milk.

CAKE — LADY (D)
(Mrs. Mitchell's, American)

Ingredients:

¼ lb. butter
¾ lb. rolled white sugar
1 lb. self-raising flour
Whites of 4 eggs
1 cup lukewarm water
1 lemon

(But if you are out of self-raising flour use ordinary flour, but add 2 tsps. Royal baking-powder, this latter to be added just before the last whites of eggs are put in)

Beat the butter to a cream and gradually add the sugar; then, slowly beating all the time, add the cup of lukewarm water; then take half the quantity of flour and stir it in, beating vigorously. Meanwhile the whites of 4 eggs have been beaten to a stiff froth, and *half* of them is now added to the mixture, after that the remaining half of the flour is mixed in with the juice and grated rind of a lemon, and lastly the rest of the whites of eggs. Stir all well and bake in a moderately warm oven.

CAKE — MADEIRA

Ingredients:

4 eggs
6 oz. loaf sugar
6 oz. flour

4 oz. butter
1 lemon
½ tsp. of carbonate of soda

Whisk the eggs until they are as light as possible, then add by degrees the following ingredients: six ounces of pounded sugar, four ounces of butter, dissolved, but not heated, the grated rind of one lemon, six ounces of flour. Beat all well together; just before putting in the mould, add half a teaspoon of carbonate of soda and the juice of the lemon. Great care should be taken that the butter is perfectly mixed, and no appearance of it remains. Bake for an hour.

CAKE — NUT

Ingredients:

10 eggs
½ lb. hazel nuts or almonds
¼ lb. white sugar

2 tbsps. finest bread-crumbs
Tsp. of baking-powder

The yolks of the eggs must be mixed with sugar. Stir for twenty minutes; add the nuts or almonds (ground), bread-crumbs or finely powdered biscuit, lastly the whites well whisked, and baking-powder. Bake one hour.

CAKE — NUT (D)
(MISS LE SUEUR'S)

Ingredients:

1½ breakfast-cupfuls sugar
1 teacupful milk
1 cupful of walnuts, crushed with a
    rolling-pin or chopped

2 tbsps. butter
2 eggs
2 tsps. baking-powder
2 teacupfuls fine flour

Mix the sugar and butter to a cream, then add the eggs, well beaten, then the milk. Mix the baking-powder with the flour and stir in gently, lastly add the walnuts. Stir all well and put into a well-buttered mould and bake in a moderate oven for an hour. Walnuts, hickory nuts, and butter-nuts are best, but other nuts will do.

CAKE — PARKIN (D)

Ingredients:

2 lb. sifted oatmeal
½ lb. coarse brown sugar
Ground ginger

2 lb. treacle
½ lb. butter
A little brandy

The ground ginger should be added to flavour, and the mixture baked in a very slow oven, in flat cakes the size of a saucer, or larger.

CAKE — PLUM
(COPIED FROM MRS. SPENCE'S RECIPE BOOK)

Ingredients:

1 lb. flour
1 lb. butter
1 lb. brown sugar
2 lb. currants
1 lb. raisins
½ lb. candied peel

2 oz. mixed spices—cloves, cinna-
    mon, ginger, nutmeg, allspice
8 eggs
1 wineglass of brandy
20 drops essence of almonds

Beat the butter to a cream; then add sugar and eggs, well beaten; then spice and candied fruit and brandy; adding flour last. Beat all together very well, and at the last add gradually one packet of baking-powder. Put into buttered mould. Bake one hour and a half.

CAKE — POUND
(MRS. DANIEL CLOETE'S BOOK)

Ingredients:

1 lb. of flour
A cup of currants
2 lb. loaf sugar
½ lb. butter
4 eggs

1 breakfastcup of milk
¼ nutmeg (grated)
1 tsp. baking-powder
Some citron preserve (cut small)

Mix butter, whipped to a cream, with sugar; then yolks, then flour, etc.; lastly whites, whisked to a stiff froth. The baking powder to be mixed dry with the flour. Bake 1½ hours in moderate oven. *Good.*

CAKE — POUND
(Old Cape Recipe. Mrs. Reitz's)

Ingredients:

12 eggs
1 lb. butter
1 lb. sugar
1 lb. flour

Tsp. of mixed cinnamon, nartje-peel (tangerin eorange), dried and powdered; and some nut-meg

Whisk the eggs (whites and yolks) separately. Stir the butter to a cream; add dry sifted sugar, then yolks, well whisked, then flour and spices, previously well mixed, and lastly, the whites. Have a well-buttered mould, dusted with fine biscuit; a buttered paper on the top of mould. Bake in a moderate oven for two hours.

CAKE — PRUSSIAN
(Berg River)

Ingredients:

8 eggs
1 lb. flour
1 lb. white sugar

250 sweet almonds
20 bitter almonds
Wineglass of brandy

Whisk the yolks and whites separately. Blanch and pound the almonds. Beat the yolks and sugar together; then the whites; add the flour, and lastly, the almonds. Bake one hour and a half. *Very good cake.*

CAKE — QUEEN

Ingredients:

1 lb. butter
1 tbsp. orange-flower water
1 lb. white sugar

10 eggs
1½ lb. of flour
½ lb. almonds

Beat butter to a cream; add orange-flower water; then the sugar (pounded), the eggs beaten very light, a pound and a half of finest flour. Beat all well together; add half a pound of blanched almonds. Butter tins lined with paper; put in the mixture an inch and a half deep. Bake in a quick oven one hour.

CAKE — RIBBON (D)
(Mrs. Griffiths's of Port Elizabeth)

Ingredients:

¾ lb. sugar
1 lb. flour
½ lb. butter
¼ tsp. soda

6 eggs
1 tsp. cream of tartar
1 large cupful milk

Beat the butter to a cream with the sugar. Add the eggs, one at a time, the milk alternately with the flour sifted with the soda and cream of tartar. Mix all well together, and flavour with vanilla essence. Divide this quantity into 3 equal parts, and pour into baking tins, leaving one tin plain, colouring a second with cochineal, and the third with a sixpenny cake of chocolate, grated and dissolved in half a cup of milk extra, stirred into it. When all are baked, set to cool, and when nearly cold cut in layers; while the cakes are cooling make the icing. Before quite cold build the layers of cake together, the icing between the slices, so that the plain cake, the pink and the brown come alternately, and pour the rest of the icing over the outside. (*See* Mrs. Griffiths's Icing.)

CAKE — SILVER

Ingredients:

2 cups of flour	Whites of 4 eggs
½ cup of butter	1 tsp. cream of tartar
1¼ cup of sugar	1 tsp. soda
½ cup milk	20 drops essence of almonds

Make the same as Golden Cake; can be made at the same time.

CAKE — SODA
(MRS. MYBURGH'S)

Ingredients:

1 lb. flour	Tsp. of soda
½ lb. sugar	Tsp. of cream of tartar
¼ lb. butter	Some lemon peel (grated), or cinna-
3 eggs	mon.
½ lb. currants	1 pint of milk

First rub sugar and butter well together. Mix the soda, etc., dry with the flour and currants; then rub that with butter and sugar; lastly add the pint of milk. Put into the oven immediately, and bake an hour and a quarter. *Very good and cheap.*

CAKE — SPONGE
(MRS. VAN DER BYL'S)

Ingredients:

10 eggs	The rind of a lemon (grated) and
The weight of 9 eggs in sugar	the juice
	½ lb. of flour

Whisk the whites and yolks separately. Crush the sugar; whisk it with the whites; then add the flour, and lastly, the yolks. Just before putting in the oven, add the lemon. Put into well-buttered mould, dusted with fine biscuit. Bake in a moderate oven with a paper over it. *This makes a very large cake, or two small ones.*

CAKE — A GOOD SPONGE (D)

Ingredients:

7 eggs.
Their weight in sugar
The weight of 3 in flour

Juice of 1 lemon
Pinch of salt

Carefully break the eggs, and whisk the whites and yolks separately. Use castor-sugar (if it is not at hand, roll the sugar on your pastry board *till fine*); the flour should be slightly warmed; have the mould ready, well buttered and dusted with finely-pounded biscuit.

Mix the sugar with the stiffly-whisked whites, next add the yolks and then the flour and lemon-juice. Pour the mixture into the mould and bake in a moderate oven one hour, putting a buttered paper over the mould. Put the cake for baking at the bottom of the oven and *do not open the door* for half an hour or more after putting it in. *Be careful not to slam the oven-door,* or the cake will go down.

I have read somewhere that the way confectioners get a smooth outside to their sponge-cakes is by (after greasing the mould) dusting the inside of the mould with fine sugar and flour in equal quantities before pouring in the mixture.

CAKE — SWISS ROLL, No. 1 (D)
(MRS. BROOK-SMITH'S)

Ingredients:

1 tumbler flour
½ tumbler milk
1 tumbler white rolled sugar

2 eggs
½ tsp. soda
1 tsp. cream of tartar

Beat up the sugar and eggs together, then add the flour, mix the soda and cream of tartar in the milk and add it quickly to the flour. Bake in a buttered tin fifteen minutes. Sugar the baking-board. Turn the cake out hot on the sugared board, spread it quickly with jam and roll up quickly. It keeps its shape if rolled up when hot.

CAKE — SWISS ROLL, No. 2

Ingredients:

3 eggs
3 oz. rolled sugar

3 oz. flour
1 tsp. baking-powder

Beat the eggs and sugar together, then mix the flour with the baking-powder and add to eggs and sugar. Pour the mixture into a buttered baking dish and bake 8 or 10 minutes. Turn out on a sugared board, spread with any kind of jam and roll quickly into shape.

CAKE — TIPSY

Ingredients:

Six sponge biscuits
2 wineglasses of Van der Hum
20 almonds (blanched)

¼ lb. of apricot jam
1 pint of rich custard

Soak the sponge biscuits in the Van der Hum (*see* Liqueur, Van der Hum). Garnish them all over with almonds cut in spikes; arrange them in a pyramid shape in a glass dish, with some apricot marmalade, or any preserve you like, between. Pour over the whole a pint of good custard. (*See* Custard.) *A nice supper dish.*

CAKES.—*See also* Scones, Tea Cakes, Veal Cake, Macaroons, Oblietjies, Heuningkoek, Scraps, Apple Cake, Icing for Cakes, Tart (Dutch Potato), Tart (Walnut), Cake (Rice), Almond Cheese-cakes, Doughnuts, Koesisters, Puffs (Boston), Sandwich (Victoria), Macaroons, Meringues, Mince Pies, Mosbolletjies, Pastry, Pies, Wafels, Soetekrakeling.

CAULIFLOWER.—*See* Grated Cheese and Cauliflower.

CHARLOTTE RUSSE

Ingredients:

Some Savoy biscuits
¾ pint of good cream
¾ oz. isinglass
2 dessertsps. of Van der Hum or Curaçao

Some vanilla
1 oz. of loaf sugar
A large slice of sponge cake
1 egg

Take as many Savoy biscuits as will line the inside of your mould, which must be buttered, lightly moistening the edges of each with the beaten white of an egg, to make them hold together, and place them upright all round the sides of the mould, slightly over each other, or sufficiently close to prevent the cream from escaping. At the bottom of the mould arrange your biscuits in a star or rosette, taking care it is well covered; then set in the oven to dry. Whisk the cream with the Van der Hum (*see* Liqueur, Van der Hum), isinglass dissolved, and loaf sugar to taste. When sufficiently firm fill the inside of the Charlotte Russe, and place over it a slice of sponge-cake. Set it in a cool place or in ice, and when cold cover it with cream; ornament with chocolates, " Hundreds and thousands," crystallized cherries, etc.

CHEESECAKES — ALMOND

Ingredients:

¼ lb. sweet almonds
4 bitter almonds
3 eggs
2 oz. butter

The rind of half a lemon
A tbsp. of lemon juice
3 oz. sugar

Blanch and pound the almonds smoothly in a mortar with a little rose-water. Stir the sugar and the yolks well, warm the butter slightly, mix with the sugar, eggs, and almonds, then the juice and lemon peel. Stir well. Line some patty tins with puff paste, and fill with the mixture. Bake twenty minutes in a quick oven. *Enough for twelve Cheesecakes. Very good.*

CHEESECAKES — ALMOND, ANOTHER
(ENGLISH)

Ingredients:

¼ lb. sweet almonds	1 tbsp. of cream
6 bitter almonds	Whites of 2 eggs
¼ lb. loaf sugar	Puff paste

Blanch and pound the sweet and bitter almonds with a teaspoonful of water, then add the sugar, the cream, and whites of eggs. Mix as quickly as possible. Put into very small patty pans lined with puff paste. Bake in a warm oven for twenty minutes. *Very good.*

CHEESE DISH — RISOTTO À LA MILANAISE (D)

Put a good-sized piece of butter in a stew-pan and add a small quantity of minced onion. Let it just colour, but *not brown.* Take a handful of rice and let it cook in the butter about five minutes, adding sufficient stock to cook the rice.

When cooked add a cupful of grated cheese, and little rounds of tongue (cut slices of tongue flat and then punch out with a cutter about the size of a shilling, into rounds). Bake till brown. Put a little grated Parmesan cheese and butter on the top, and serve very hot.

CHEESE DISH — ANOTHER RISOTTO FROM GENOA (D)
(MRS. CLARK'S)

Ingredients:

4 tbsps. cooked rice	1 tbsp ham or tongue (chopped fine)
1 tbsp. of chicken or pheasant, chopped fine	1 hard-boiled egg. chopped fine
	1 small onion, chopped fine

Put a small pat of butter to get hot, and put the onion in it to cook a little first, then add the other ingredients. When serving add a spoonful of grated Parmesan cheese, salt and pepper to taste. *Serve very hot.* (Suitable for a breakfast dish).

CHEESE-STRAWS
(MRS. DANIEL CLOETE'S)

Grate two ounces of Parmesan or Cheddar cheese. Rub two ounces of butter into two ounces of flour. Add the cheese, some cayenne, and salt to taste. Mix with the yolk of an egg, roll out, and cut into strips; egg over. Bake in a quick oven. Serve very hot, nicely arrange criss-cross on a dish. Mustard to be handed round with them. *Good.*

CHEESE-STRAWS — ANOTHER KIND
(An old tried Recipe)

Ingredients:

2 oz. flour	2 oz. butter
2 oz. fine bread-crumbs	½ a saltsp. cayenne
2 oz. grated cheese	¼ saltsp. salt

Mix all well together in a paste, and roll out to a quarter of an inch in thickness. Cut into narrow strips like fingers; lay them on a buttered paper or pan. Bake in a quick oven. *Enough for eight people.*

CHEESE.—*See* Grated Cheese and Cauliflower, Pudding (Cheese) and Soufflé (Cheese).

CHESTNUT PUDDING (D)
(Mrs. Hiddingh's)

Boil 50 large chestnuts, peel and rub them through a sieve; put them in a saucepan with 1 pint of cream or milk, and 4 oz. butter; stir till the mixture thickens. As soon as it ceases to adhere to the bottom of the pot, take it off and let it cool. Beat up separately the yolks and whites of 4 eggs and mix them with the cold chestnuts; flavour with ½ teaspoonful of vanilla essence, and add a good pinch of salt. Mix thoroughly, butter a plain mould, put in the mixture, and steam for two hours. Serve hot with melted apricot jam sauce.

CHESTNUT SNOW (D)
(Miss O'Connor Eccles's)

Boil ½ lb. of chestnuts, rub them through a sieve, mix with 2 tablespoons sugar and ½ teaspoon vanilla. Line a glass dish with strawberry jam; cover this with the chestnut, sprinkle over a few brown breadcrumbs, and put slightly sweetened whipped cream, flavoured with vanilla, on top of all.

CHESTNUT CHIPOLATA (D)
(Miss Adeane's)

Skin 1 lb. of chestnuts, and put them in a stew-pan with a little *consommé*, sift a little sugar over and braise for 2 hours. Then cut sausages in pieces the size of a walnut. Also cut in squares tongue and ham, and truffles. Arrange in an entrée dish, the chestnuts at one end, ham and tongue at the other, sausages along one side, mushrooms along the other.

CHICKEN.—*See also* Fowl, Gesmoorde Hoender, Indian Pilau, and Heatherton.

29

c

CHICKEN MOULD — COLD MEAT

About one pound of the white meat of a chicken, a quarter of a pound of ham, pounded together in a mortar. Add to this two ounces of butter, three eggs, well-beaten, a quarter of a pint of whipped cream. Flavour with a little cayenne, some salt, and a little nutmeg. Mix all well together. Steam for twenty minutes. Serve with oyster or tomato sauce. *For Luncheon.*

CHICKEN — NEAPOLITAN CHICKEN À LA REINE (D)
(MRS. CLOETE'S)

Ingredients:

A fowl too old to roast	1 tsp. of brown sugar
6 large tomatoes (or canned ones)	The same of salt
½ a clove of garlic	1 oz. butter or dripping
A few sweet herbs	A strip of lemon-peel
An onion. fried in dripping	

Parboil the fowl till tender. Then take off the skin and cut the bird into nice pieces. Boil the other ingredients till the tomatoes are soft, and then press all through a colander and put back in the enamelled saucepan; lay the cut-up fowl in this and let it simmer, but not boil, for an hour. Serve as an entrée, with boiled rice.

CHICKEN RÉCHAUFFÉ
(MRS. CLOETE'S)

Take the remains of either roast or boiled fowl, cut into joints. Make a stock of the bones. Thicken with a little maizena, a piece of fresh butter, salt, pepper, a pinch of sugar, one bay leaf, a teaspoonful of tomato sauce. Put the chicken in, stew slowly for half an hour. Boil some rice in milk, season well with pepper and salt, and make a border round the dish, placing the chicken in the centre.

CHICKEN — RICE BALLS OF COLD (D)
(MISS GAPPER'S)

Ingredients :

Remains of Cold Chicken	½ lb. rice
1 quart stock	2 oz. butter

Wash the rice well, and set the stock to boil, add the rice and let it boil gently for half an hour. Now add the butter and let it simmer till the rice is dry and soft, then set the rice to get cold.

Mince the cold chicken *very fine.* Flavour with lemon-peel, salt and pepper, half a teaspoon sugar and a little butter. Shape the rice in balls, then hollow out the inside and fill with chicken. Cover the hole with rice, dip the balls in egg, sprinkle with fine bread-crumbs, and fry a light-brown in boiling fat.

CHICKEN — SCALLOPED
(MRS. DWYER'S)

Mince some chicken with some lean ham, and season with pepper, salt, and a little nutmeg, two tablespoonfuls of cream, or a little butter. Put into scallop-shells, cover with fine bread-crumbs; set them in the oven to brown, with a small bit of butter on the top of each.

CHICKEN — STEWED
(THE OLD CAPE WAY)

Ingredients:

2 young chickens	A few allspice, peppercorns, and a
2 or 3 white onions	tiny bit of mace (tied in a
1 tbsp. butter and a little clarified	muslin bag)
dripping	The yolk of an egg
1½ pints of water	Glass of white wine
1 tbsp. tomato sauce	2 tbsps. vermicelli

Truss the chickens and stuff them with fine bread-crumbs, a little butter, a slice of white onion, flavoured with a little pepper and sweet herbs. Press down the breast-bone, put a skewer through the wings, in which put the liver and gizzard, and tie the whole together.

Stew the chickens in a flat enamelled stewing-pot, with a pint and a half of water, the butter, dripping, onions (cutting two incisions on the top), and a little bag of spice. Turn the chickens *breast downwards*, let them simmer for an hour. Now remove the spices and add vermicelli and tomato sauce. Stew for half an hour, and just before serving add the yolk of an egg whipped with the wineglass of white wine, stirred into the pot, and then poured over the chickens. Serve hot. *Turkey done in this way is delicious. (See* " Broodkluitjies " *to go with this.)*

CHILLI VINEGAR

Take green chillies, prick and sprinkle with salt, put into a wide-mouthed bottle; pour on them some vinegar in which a few small onions, bits of ginger, and coriander seeds have been boiled. Let it cool before putting over the chillies. Cork well. *This is very good with cold meat.*

CHIPOLATA — A DELICIOUS PUDDING
(MRS. HIDDINGH'S)

Soak a quarter of an ounce of gelatine in a little water for a quarter of an hour. Make a custard of a pint of milk, two eggs, two table-spoonfuls sugar. Add gelatine before adding eggs and sugar.

Take nine sponge biscuits; slice thinly; soak in half a wineglass of Van der Hum, or the syrup in which peaches have been preserved.

Garnish a buttered porcelain mould with little bits of citron preserve, or Cape gooseberry; then put in a layer of soaked biscuits. Have ready any kind of preserve, such as yellow peaches (preserved in brandy), water-melon, or ginger (cut small); put in a layer of preserve; then some more soaked sponge biscuits; pour over the whole the custard (which must be warm), to fill the mould, and let it stand overnight. If ice is handy, this pudding is greatly improved by being iced.

CHUTNEY
(Mrs. Coleman's)

Ingredients:

2 tbsps. apricot jam	2 dessertsps. pounded ginger
1 dessertsp. salt	6 sour apples
2 dessertsps. cayenne	2 large onions

Boil the apples and onions, then mash fine, and mix with the other ingredients. Put in bottles and cork.

CHUTNEY — ANOTHER INDIAN
(Mrs. Lockhart's)

Ingredients:

1 lb. dried apples, or apricots	¼ lb. red chillies
1 lb. raisins (stoned)	1 lb. soft sugar
1 lb. onions	2 oz. salt
1 lb. ginger	4 oz. garlic

Mix all these ingredients. After having been pounded in a stone jar with four quarts of water, set it in the *sun* for a week. As the vinegar gets absorbed, more should be added. Bottle and cork. *Keep some months before using.*

CHUTNEY — APPLE
(Mrs. Jackson's, Old Indian)

Ingredients:

2 soup plates of sour apples (sliced)	1 large breakfast-cup of stoned raisins
¼ lb. dried apricots, soaked in 1 quart of vinegar till soft	3 tbsps. coriander seeds
5 large onions	1 lb. sugar
1 garlic	½ lb. salt
1 soup plate of fresh red chillies	½ lb. ginger
	3 tbsps. of mustard seeds

All these ingredients to be bruised fine (dry). The garlic and onions *minced*, the raisins *stoned*. The other ingredients to be well mixed. The *whole* to be boiled in three quarts of vinegar till it looks clear. *This is a most delicious Chutney.*

CHUTNEY — ANOTHER INDIAN
(AUNT FANNY'S)

Ingredients:

3 lb. quince, apricots, or apples	2 lb. salt
½ lb. dried chillies	1 lb. raisins
1 lb. sugar	¼ lb. garlic
¼ lb. ginger	4 quarts vinegar

Peel and cut the quinces, apples, or apricots; boil in three bottles of vinegar till soft; mash in all the sugar and other ingredients; then add the rest of the vinegar. Cork. *Will keep for years and improves by age.*

CHUTNEY — ANOTHER
(FROM A BENGAL RECIPE)

Ingredients:

1½ lb. sugar	¼ lb. dried chillies
¾ lb. salt	¾ lb. mustard seeds
¼ lb. garlic	¾ lb. stoned raisins
¼ lb. onions	30 large, unripe, sour apples
¾ lb. ginger	2 quarts of vinegar

The sugar made into syrup; the garlic, onions, ginger finely pounded; mustard seeds dried; apples peeled, cored, sliced, and boiled in half the vinegar. When the apples are cold, put in a large pan, and mix the rest of the ingredients in the remainder of the vinegar (hot), till the whole is mixed. Cork well. *This recipe was given by a native to an English lady who had long resided in India.*

CHUTNEY.—*See* Quince Sambal.

CLARET CUP
(MRS. FLEMING'S)

Ingredients:

1 quart of claret	1 tbsp. of sugar
½ wineglass of sherry or Van der Hum	A little nutmeg
½ wineglass of brandy	A sprig of borage or slice of cucumber
A squeeze of lemon and some peel	

Put the whole into a jug with a few lumps of ice. When wanted add a bottle of soda water.

COCOANUT DROPS
(SWELLENDAM)

To a grated cocoanut, add half its weight in sugar, and the white of one egg beaten stiff. Drop small pieces on a buttered paper; sift sugar over them. Bake fifteen minutes in a slow oven.

COCOANUT ICE

Take an ordinary-sized cocoanut (fresh), grated quite fine, the white of one egg beaten stiff, two tablespoons of sifted loaf sugar, a few drops of rose-water. Make into sugar-loaf shapes; set in oven for a few minutes. It must not be brown, but crisp and white outside, soft and melting in the centre. *Very good. See* Ice (Cocoanut).

COFFEE FOR TRAVELLING OR PICNICS

Take one pound of the best Java coffee, have it roasted to a rich dark-brown in an American coffee roaster, at home. Grind whilst warm. To one pound of coffee take one quarter of a pound of chicory. The best pot for making coffee for ordinary use is the common black tin coffee-pot, with a bag made of coarse flannel, the shape of a jelly-bag. Take one large breakfast cup of ground coffee pour the coffee into the bag, taking care first to have the pot warmed; on this pour three cups of *boiling* water. Keep the pot on the stove or coals, let coffee drain through the bag twice, then put into bottles and cork immediately. This will keep, if well corked and made *quickly*, for a fortnight, and is most excellent for picnics when one tablespoon added to a cup of *boiling* milk will be found as good as any freshly-made coffee. For ordinary use, when not so much milk would be used, add four cups of water instead of three to a breakfast-cup of ground coffee mixed with chicory.

COLD MEAT.—*See* Note at end of C.

CONDIMENT.—*See* Blatjang, Pickle, Chutney, Cucumber Samba, Quince Sambal, Sauce (Horse radish).

TO COOL WINE, ETC., WHERE ICE IS NOT TO BE HAD

Stand your decanter or bottles in a current of air with wet cloth round them.

COOL DRINKS.—*See also* Lemon Syrup, Ginger Pop.

COOL DRINKS — GINGER BEER, No. 1 (D)
(Mrs. Lowndes's)

Ingredients:

6 gallons water	6 oz. stick ginger
6 lb. sugar	1 oz. cream of tartar
6 lemons	1 tbsp. yeast

Cut the lemon in slices, and put in 1 gallon of the water. Boil with the ginger for 10 minutes, then add the rest of the water, sugar, cream of tartar, and yeast. Let it stand 24 hours, with a cloth over it, and then bottle.

Ingredients:

7 lb. white sugar
2 oz. cream of tartar

1 lb. bruised ginger
2 oz. tartaric acid

Boil the sugar and ginger with about as much water as will fill an anker (i.e., 6 or 7 gallons). When cold mix the cream of tartar and the tartaric acid in a cup and stir well into the liquid. Let it stand 3 or 4 days, then bottle. In a week's time it will be fit for use.

CREAM — APPLE
(MRS. CLOETE'S)

Ingredients:

12 apples
½ lb. sugar

2 eggs

Boil twelve apples very soft, mix the pulp with half a pound of white sugar; whip the whites of two eggs to a stiff froth, add to the apples. Beat all well together, heap on a glass dish.

CREAM CHEESE (D)

Put a dry cloth in the mould and fill it with thick cream, when it must remain undisturbed till it stiffens in about 2 days, then turn into a fresh cloth and replace in mould. Do the same daily till firm enough, then sprinkle a little salt on it and fold in a cloth for 2 or 3 days in a cool place, when it will be ready for use.

CREAM IN MOULDS
(MRS. ETHERIDGE'S)

Ingredients:

1 oz. isinglass
1 pint cream
2 tbsps. of brandy

Sugar to taste
4 tbsps. of strawberry or apricot
jam

Soak the ounce of isinglass in cold water, add a little boiling milk, stir till nearly cold. Then add four tablespoonfuls of jam to the cream; add to the isinglass, stirring till nice and smooth. Add brandy and sugar. Pour into a porcelain mould and turn out when cold and firm. *Very good.*

CREAM — CHOCOLATE

Ingredients:

½ pint of cream
A little milk
2 oz. chocolate, dissolved in a little
warm water or milk

4 oz. powdered white sugar
1 oz. isinglass dissolved in boiling
water
The juice of half a lemon

Whisk up the cream to a stiff froth, then add the sugar, chocolate, lemon juice, and isinglass. Mix all well together and pour into a mould. Let it stand till set. Dip the mould in hot water for half a minute before turning out.

35

CREAM — CHOCOLATE ICED
(MISS BONNIE CLOETE'S)

Ingredients:

3 oz. grated chocolate	3 eggs
1 pint of milk	½ cup of cream
4 oz. sugar	

Dissolve the chocolate in a pint of milk on the fire with the sugar, then add the yolks of the eggs well whisked. Stir as you would a custard, and when cool add the cream well whipped. Put into a mould, and ice.

CREAM — COFFEE

Ingredients:

½ pint of very strong coffee	1 pint milk
1 tsp. vanilla essence	Tbsp. of rich cream
1 oz. Nelson's gelatine	3 oz. lump sugar

Soak the gelatine in the coffee. When nearly dissolved, place it in an enamelled saucepan with the milk, cream, sugar, and vanilla essence; stir over the fire till almost boiling, then pour into a wetted mould. Let it set overnight.

CREAM — DEVONSHIRE

Strain new milk from the cow into large flat pans, or tins; let it stand for twenty-four hours in winter, twelve in summer, to allow the cream to rise; then place the pans on a hot dresser, or gas stove not too hot; let it warm gently till *just on the point of boiling*, then take the pans off the stove. Set it aside to cool. When cold skim the cream. Heap it on a dish, and serve.

CREAM — DUTCH
(MRS. DWYER'S)

Ingredients:

1 pint milk	1 glass brandy
1 gill of cream	1 oz. chopped lemon or citron
4 oz. loaf sugar	preserve
¼ lb. ground rice	The juice of an orange
1 egg	

Boil milk, sugar, and ground rice together until the rice is quite soft; then add the egg (stirring all the time), then the cream and other ingredients. Put into a mould to set. Serve. You may melt a table-spoonful of apricot marmalade in a little hot water, add a wineglass of brandy, and serve with this cream, but *it is very good without.*

CREAM — FRUIT — IN A MOULD
(Miss Bonnie Cloete's)

Ingredients:

¼ packet gelatine, well soaked in cold water
½ pint boiling milk

1 pint of cream
4 tbsps. apricot jam, or any fruit jelly you like

Pour the milk boiling on the gelatine, whisk up the cream and fruit jelly, add the milk and gelatine; pour into a buttered mould. Turn out when cold in a glass dish. *Enough for eight people.*

CREAM — HONEYCOMB
(Mrs. G. Ebden's)

Ingredients:

1 quart of milk
1 oz. white sugar
3 eggs

½ oz. gelatine
1 tsp. vanilla

Dissolve the gelatine (which should be previously soaked) over the fire, with the milk and sugar; then stir in the yolks of the eggs (previously well beaten), and boil the whole mixture *only once.* Take off the fire, stir in the whites (which have been whisked to a stiff froth) and the essence of vanilla. Put into a mould, and turn out next day.

CREAM — ISINGLASS
(Mrs. Etheridge's)

Ingredients:

1 oz. isinglass
1 pint cream
2 tbsps. brandy

2 tbsps. sugar
Some apricot jam

Soak one ounce of isinglass in a little cold water; add a cup of boiling milk, and stir till cold. Then mix four spoonfuls of jam with the cream, stirring the whole until nice and smooth; then add the sugar and brandy. *Good.*

CREAM — ITALIAN
(From a recipe given by an English lady who had once lived in Italy)

Ingredients:

1 cup of cream
Apricot jam

Whites of 2 eggs
White (castor) sugar

Whisk the cream and two spoonfuls of apricot jam well; strain through a milk sieve. Whisk the whites of two eggs to a stiff froth mix with the cream; and lastly, stir in one or two spoonfuls of sugar, according to taste. Will fill half a dozen or more glasses. *It is most delicious, and not too rich.*

37

CREAM — LEMON

Ingredients:

1 quart cream	1½ oz. isinglass
2 large lemons	A pinch of salt
12 oz. loaf sugar	

Infuse into a pint of the cream the thin rind of the lemons.

Dissolve the isinglass, or soak it in a little cold milk; add the sugar; then put the saucepan on the fire; do not let it boil, but keep near simmering till the sugar and isinglass are quite dissolved; then stir in the other pint of cream. Strain the mixture in a basin through a milk sieve. When nearly cold, stir in the juice of two lemons. Pour into an oiled or buttered mould, and leave in a cool place before turning out.

CREAM — LEMON SOLID
(A SIMILAR RECIPE)

Ingredients:

1 quart of new milk	1 oz. gelatine
¾ lb. sugar	2 or 3 lemons

Soak the gelatine in some of the milk for a quarter of an hour; add to it the sugar and rind of lemon cut very thin; put the whole in a saucepan, and let it boil a few minutes, then stir in the remainder of the cold milk. When nearly cold, squeeze in the juice of the lemons. It is better made the day before, and put into a wetted or oiled mould till cold.

CREAM — ORANGE
(MRS. FLEMING'S)

Ingredients:

1 quart milk	Rind of 2 oranges
3 eggs	1 oz. gelatine
4 oz. sugar	Juice of 1 lemon

Make a custard of the milk and eggs, stir till it thickens. Dissolve the gelatine (previously soaked in cold water) in a little warm water, add to it the juice of a lemon, then stir in the custard; put into a buttered mould, and set to ice.

CREAM — STONE

Ingredients:

Marmalade, Jam or preserve	1 wineglass of sherry
¼ oz. gelatine	Milk may be substituted for cream,
1 oz. loaf sugar	but, if so, an egg and a tsp. of
1 pint cream	butter should be added

Cover the bottom of a pie-dish with a thin layer of marmalade (or jam). Stir into the pint of cream a quarter of an ounce of gelatine previously dissolved, and one ounce of loaf sugar; let it boil a few minutes, stir all the time. Strain, and when cooled add a wineglass of sherry, then pour over the preserve. If milk is used instead of cream add one teaspoonful of butter, and when boiled whisk the yolk of an egg into the mixture, then pour it over the marmalade.

CREAM — STRAWBERRY

Ingredients:

2 lb. ripe strawberries	12 oz. sugar
1 quart of cream or milk	1 oz. isinglass

Pour the cream or milk into a stew-pan, add sugar and isinglass to dissolve, not allowing the mixture to boil; then strain into a basin and stir until nearly cold. Add the fruit, which has been previously passed through a hair-sieve, oil the mould, and pour in the cream. Allow it to stand until it is quite firm.

CREAM — SWISS
(MRS. D. CLOETE'S)

Ingredients:

1 quart of cream or milk	8 tbsps. of maizena
12 oz. of sugar	½ lb. macaroons
2 lemons	A small stick of cinnamon

Set the cream, or rich milk, on the fire (keeping a little to moisten the maizena), add sugar, and cinnamon, and maizena; let it boil for five minutes. Pour into a basin; when nearly cold, add the juice of the lemons. Take half the macaroons and cover the bottom of a glass dish, pour over the cream; another layer of macaroons, another of cream, and so on. This pudding should be made the day before.

CROQUETTES OF CHICKEN
(MRS. DWYER'S)

Ingredients:

1 lb. cooked chicken	1 blade of mace
½ lb. of mixed mushrooms	2 eggs
Truffles and ham (or tongue)	Bread-crumbs
A little pepper	Some rich stock

Mince fine about one pound of cooked chicken with mushroom, tongue (or ham), and truffles; season with the spices. Have some rich stock reduced by boiling till quite thick, stir well together. Spread it on a dish an inch thick, cover with buttered paper, and set it to cool. Divide into nice little balls, dip in egg, roll in breadcrumbs and fry a light brown.

CROQUETTES OF FISH

Take any cold boiled fish, pound it well, season with salt and cayenne. Put one ounce of butter in a stew pan, add two ounces flour, one gill of milk, stir over the fire till it thickens, and boils, and is smooth; add to it one pound of the cold fish, one teaspoonful of anchovy or Worcestershire sauce. Stir all together, and turn all into plate to cool. When cool make into shapes, dip into egg, and roll in bread-crumbs. Fry in *hot* fat, and serve with fried parsley.

CROQUETTES OF RICE

Ingredients:

1 oz. rice	5 oz. sugar
1 quart of milk	A few bitter almonds
Rind of a lemon	

Boil all this well together; when cold form into balls. Scoop out and put apricot jam in the centre, roll in egg, and dust with powdered biscuit. Fry in hot lard.

CAKE — RICE

Ingredients:

½ lb. of butter, whipped to cream	¼ lb. of ground rice
1 lb. of loaf sugar	½ lb. of flour
7 eggs—whites of 4	Essence of lemon

Mix the sugar and butter, then the yolks, then rice and flour, lastly whites and flavouring. Bake an hour and a half with buttered paper over mould.

CRUST.—*See* Pie Crust, Puff Paste, Pastry.

CUCUMBER — SAVOURY

Pare and scoop out the seeds of a moderate sized cucumber. Grate one tablespoonful of cheese, one of breadcrumbs, a little chopped parsley, chives, pepper, salt, butter. Stuff cucumber and bake in the oven for half an hour. Have sauce made thus: one tablespoonful of cheese, teaspoonful flour, teaspoonful butter, half a teaspoonful of mustard, little pepper and salt. Stir in the saucepan with a tablespoonful of milk; stir till thick. Pour this over cucumber, cover with breadcrumbs, brown, and serve.

CURRY OF COLD MEAT
(MY RECIPE)

Take one large onion, cut small, fry a nice brown. To a tablespoonful of butter or dripping mixed, add two green apples or a large quince (if not at hand, take two or three tomatoes), cut in slices; simmer with a large tablespoonful of curry-powder and the fried onion, a tablespoon of vinegar or lemon, a dessertspoonful of sugar, half a cup of stock and a little milk. Cut up some cold meat in nice little pieces, lay in this mixture, and simmer for an hour or more till the meat is thoroughly flavoured with the curry paste. Serve with hot boiled rice. Any cold boiled or roast meat will do.

N.B.—Half an ounce of tamarinds, soaked in boiling water and strained, gives a delicious flavour to curry, and may always be substituted for vinegar.

CURRY — CHICKEN
(OUR CAPE WAY)

Ingredients:

1 fowl	2 tbsps. of vinegar or 2 sour apples
1½ tbsps. curry-powder	1 oz. butter
1 tsp. of sugar	2 onions sliced and browned in
¼ tsp. salt	butter or fat

The fowl must not be more than twelve months old, and must be killed the day before cooking. Cut into small joints. Mix the onion with the curry-powder, vinegar, salt, sugar, and butter to a paste; lay on the chicken. Cover the pot and let it simmer, or stew gently for an hour, then stir well. If dry, add a little water. A tablespoon of tomato sauce or lemon in half a cup of milk, stirred in shortly before serving, is an improvement, but it will be found excellent without. Serve with boiled rice. *Sufficient as an entrée for six or eight people.*

Some people fry the meat and onion together till brown; but from experience I find it best to do the onions first, and then let all *steam* with the chicken.

CURRY — COLD (D)
(THE BLUES)

Take some carrots, onions, celery, apples, tomatoes, and a bunch of herbs. Fry all a nice brown, then add curry-powder, curry-paste, and flour to taste. Fry these also. When that is cooled add some chutney and some good jellied stock (or a good lump of glaze, or a small pot of Liebig's extract of meat). Boil well together, and pass through a tammy; the sauce is then ready. If meat already cooked is to be used for this curry, cut it up in rather large dice, add to the sauce, and boil up; and then turn out into the dish to be used next day. But if uncooked meat is used, it will require to be fried a nice brown and cooked in the curry-sauce for an hour. (To be served with cold boiled rice round it, which can be garnished with red and green chillies, if liked.)

CURRY — CUCUMBER
(A Cape Dish)

Take four large cucumbers that are turning *yellow;* peel carefully (be particular that no bitter be left). Take out the seeds, cut in halves across, or if large in three pieces, stuff with forcemeat, made as follows: one pound of mutton (fresh or cold) *minced,* one slice of bread soaked in milk, one egg, a little salt and pepper, a dessertspoonful of curry-powder. Mix well together, stuff the cucumber with this. Then take two large onions, fry a nice brown; make a paste of curry-powder, one ounce, one teaspoonful of sugar, one tablespoonful of vinegar, a cup of stock, a good tablespoonful of dripping (butter is better); simmer in a flat stewing-pot. Arrange the stuffed cucumber in this, and let it simmer on a moderate heat for two hours. Serve with boiled rice. (This is a nice *entrée* or lunch dish.)

CURRY — A GOOD MUTTON

Ingredients:

2 lb. of mutton (thick rib makes a nice dish)	1 tbsp. of vinegar
2 large onions	1 tbsp. of good curry-powder (if not sure of the curry-powder add a teaspoonful of Indian curriy-paste)
2 sour apples or tomatoes	
2 tsps. of sugar	
1 tsp. of salt	

Cut the mutton in nice little pieces. Fry the mutton and onion a nice brown, cut the apple or tomato in slices, mix with curry-powder and other ingredients; stir all well together. Simmer for two hours gently. Serve with boiled rice. Cold meat cut in slices, and simmered in this mixture of curry, etc., for two hours, does very well.

CURRY — ANOTHER MUTTON
(This was taught me by an Indian cook)

Take three pounds of mutton out of the leg; cut into small square pieces, and put into the pot. Slice up a large onion thinly; put that on top of the meat. Now make a paste of two tablespoonfuls of curry-powder, one tablespoonful of brown sugar, two tablespoonfuls of vinegar. If apples are in season, slice up two or three and add to it. Stir all together and put this on top of the sliced onions. Shut up the pot; let it simmer gently. *No water to be added.* After an hour, stir all well together. Let it simmer gently another hour. Just before serving, add half a cupful of milk and a tablespoonful of tomato sauce. Serve with rice.

CURRY — VEGETABLE

Chop four onions and four apples, put them in a pan with a quarter of a pound of butter, let them fry a light brown; add a tablespoonful of curry-powder, a little stock, and some salt.

Parboil six large potatoes whole; cut them up, and put them with the other ingredients. Let all stew gently for an hour. Cover the pot. *Vegetable marrow makes a very nice curry.*

CURRY.—*See also* Eggs (Curried), Bobotie, Sasaties, Soup (Curry), and recipe for Rice.

CUCUMBER SAMBAL
(A Malay Dish)

Ingredients:

2 young cucumbers	Vinegar, or Lemon
Cayenne	Salt
Soy	A spring onion

Peel your cucumbers; then cut off the green fleshy part, leaving out all the seeds. Cut up this in thin shreds, also some spring onions; add cayenne, or green chilli; a few tablespoonfuls of lemon juice, or vinegar, about a teaspoonful of soy. If eaten with fish, add some anchovy sauce.

CUSTARD IN CUPS

Ingredients:

1 pint of milk	Cinnamon, or 20 drops of vanilla
4 eggs	essence
	3 oz. white sugar

Boil the milk in an enamelled saucepan, with the sugar and any flavouring you prefer (if vanilla essence, put it in when the custard is made); let the milk steep by the side of the fire till quite seasoned. Whisk the eggs well, bring milk to boiling point, then strain into a basin. When it has cooled a *little*, stir in the eggs. Strain this mixture into a jug; place this jug in a saucepan of boiling water over the fire; keep stirring the custard *one way* until it thickens, but on no account allow it to reach boiling point or it will curdle and be lumpy. Take it off the fire, stir in a wineglass of brandy (if liked). Time—half an hour to infuse lemon-peel or flavouring; about ten minutes to stir the custard. *Sufficient for eight glasses.*

CUSTARD — BAKED (D)

Ingredients:

4 yolks of egg to a pint of milk
Spoon of sugar

One-inch stick of cinnamon (or a little vanilla bean) and some lemon-peel

The trimmings of the paste which remain over from the crust of a fruit pie I generally use up by rolling them out to line a pie-dish in which I am going to bake a custard, buttering the hollow of the dish and damping the sides to make the paste adhere; it should go well down the sides. *We want the custard solid!* and the paste is to absorb the superfluous fluid. As the crust is not to be eaten it is of no consequence if it is sodden.

Put the milk on the fire with the sugar, cinnamon and lemon-peel. Bring *nearly* to the boil; beat the yolks well and stir into the hot milk, then strain into the pie-dish lined with the paste. Bake in a moderate oven for three-quarters of an hour, and let it stand to get cold.

CUTLETS

Trim your cutlets carefully; lay them in a little milk, which makes the meat white and tender. (Fresh meat laid for five or six hours in a little milk will be found nice and tender.) Have ready some fine bread-crumbs, nutmeg, pepper, salt, lard, or dripping.

Roll the cutlets in egg and breadcrumbs, sprinkle with pepper, salt and nutmeg, fry in hot lard. Serve with mashed potatoes. When tomatoes are plentiful, boil about a dozen with a small piece of onion, strain, add a pat of butter, and serve round the cutlets.

CUTLETS AND GREEN PEAS

Ingredients:

3 lb. of the best end of neck of lamb
Bread-crumbs
2 eggs

Some beef or mutton dripping or lard
Pepper, salt, a little nutmeg

Cut the cutlets from the best end of the neck. Chop off the thick part of the chine bone; trim the cutlets neatly by taking off the skin and greater part of the fat, and scraping the upper end of the bone perfectly clean. Brush each cutlet with well-beaten yolk of egg, sprinkle them with fine bread-crumbs seasoned with pepper, salt and nutmeg. After this dip them separately into clarified butter, sprinkle more crumbs over them, then fry a nice brown in a frying-pan with either butter, or lard, or dripping. Serve with a nicely-boiled dish of green peas arranged in a pyramid in the middle of the dish. Can also be served with tomato sauce. Time, eight or ten minutes for cooking.

CUTLETS IN PAPER (D)

Pare and cut up the cutlets neatly. Soak them in egg and roll them in fine bread-crumbs, to which is added a little grating of nutmeg, pepper and salt. Butter some sheets of cooking paper and fold the cutlet in it, leaving the end of each bone sticking out. Bake in a hot oven in a cutlet-dish, or they may be done in a baking tin or an enamelled dish 2 inches deep.

CUTLETS — STEWED
(A HOMELY, NICE DISH)

Cut and trim your cutlets, roll them in fine bread-crumbs flavoured with nutmeg, pepper, salt, the tiniest shred of onion; lay them in a flat pot in layers. Cover the pot well, let them simmer for an hour. Put *no water*. A little before serving, stir in a little cup of stock, a spoonful of tomato sauce, and a tiny pat of butter. Let the cutlets simmer in this for a few minutes and then serve.

COLD MEAT (TO DO UP).—*See* Chicken Réchauffé, Chicken Mould, Chicken (Scalloped), Croquettes, Curry, Fowl (Fricasseed), Fowl (Sauté), Fritters, Hash, Kedgeree, Mutton Chops in Batter, Patties, Pudding (Roman), Pudding (Tomato), Pudding (Meat), Ragout, Rissoles, Shape (Cold Meat Toad-in-the-Hole).

D

DELICIOSA
(MRS. FLEMING'S)

Ingredients:

4 oz. almonds	½ tsp. cinnamon
3 stale penny sponge-cakes	Some grated orange peel
8 oz. white sugar	Whites of 2 or 3 eggs

Pound the almonds, crumble the sponge biscuits, etc., mix with the whites of three eggs well whisked. Bake in small patty tins till a golden colour, in a brisk oven, for a quarter of an hour or less. Have ready some whipped cream, with any small preserved fruit, put a teaspoonful on each, with a little preserve in the centre.

DICK'S DISH
(MRS. ETHERIDGE'S)

Put slices of cooked or uncooked meat in a pie-dish. Put mustard, pepper and salt on each piece according to taste, with plenty of Harvey's Sauce and a slice of onion. Cover the meat with a good rich gravy (made by boiling stock and thickening with a little flour), then cover the top with a rich crust of mashed potatoes. Bake in an oven.

DOUGHNUTS
(MRS. CLOETE'S)

Ingredients:

¾ lb. flour
½ lb. sugar
1 tsp. cream of tartar

1 tsp. soda
2 eggs
1¼ small cups of milk

Mix so that it will drop out of a spoon, but not flow. Fry in lard.

DUCK — HASHED

Ingredients :

Remains of cold roast duck
Little more than a pint of weak
    stock or water
1 onion
1 oz. butter

Thickening of butter and flour
Salt and cayenne to taste
½ tsp. of minced lemon-peel
Dessertsp. of lemon-juice
½ glass of port wine

Cut the duck into nice joints, and put the trimmings in a stew-pan. Slice and fry the onions in a little dripping, add these to the trimmings; strain the liquor, thicken it with flour and butter, season with cayenne and salt, add remaining ingredients; boil it up and skim well. Lay in this gravy the remaining pieces of duck; let them get thoroughly hot by the side of the fire, but do not boil; they should soak in the gravy for half an hour. Garnish with sippets of fried bread.

DUMPLINGS — BAKED APPLE

Ingredients:

6 apples
¾ lb. suet crust

Sugar to taste

Pare and take out the cores of the apples without dividing them. Make a suet crust as follows: Half a pound of suet, cut exceedingly fine, and mixed with a pound of flour, a little salt, and half a pint of water, and rolled out. This crust can be much improved by making as in recipe for Pastry (Suet). Sweeten the apples with moist sugar roll them in crust, taking care to join the paste neatly; when they are formed into round balls, bake them on a tin for half an hour or more. Arrange on a dish, and sift over with white sugar. Time, about three-quarters of an hour.

DUMPLINGS — GERMAN MILK
(KLUITJIES, FROM A RECIPE OVER A HUNDRED YEARS OLD)

Ingredients:

1 quart of milk
2 tbsps. butter

1½ cups flour
3 eggs

Boil half the milk, stir in the butter, then add the flour, stirring all the while on the fire till quite a thick paste. When cool, beat up the three eggs into it. Boil the other half-bottle of milk, and take with a teaspoon little pieces of the dough; put them into the milk, and boil for a quarter of an hour.

A delicious old-fashioned German dish was made in the following way: A young fowl, cut in small joints, was fried with some butter and sliced onion to a nice brown; about a pint of water was added *when brown*, and some red chillies. In this gravy was stirred some of the above *Milk Kluitjies* a few minutes before serving.

DUMPLINGS — RICE
(VERY OLD CAPE RECIPE. CAPE NAME, RYSKLUITJIES)

Ingredients:

1 lb. rice	3 dessertsps. melted butter
3 eggs	Sugar „
3 tbsps. flour	Cinnamon

Boil the rice as for curry, only not quite so dry; let it cool; mix with flour, eggs, and butter; roll in sugar-loaf shapes (about eight or nine from this quantity), dust with flour, and put into boiling water. When done, it rises to the top. Serve with sugar and cinnamon. Time about 10 minutes.

In most Cape Dutch houses this dish is eaten with meat, and generally made when a corned brisket of beef is boiled. Instead of mixing melted butter with the rice, some of the fat is taken from the stock in which the beef is boiling; and when the dumplings are ready, the meat is taken out about ten minutes before dinner, and the dumplings are boiled in the stock, and served with sugar. Whether from the Germans or the Dutch, most colonists who are not of English parentage, are very fond of sweet things with meat—such as stewed fruit, sweet potatoes, or parsnips done with sugar.

DUMPLINGS — RICE

Take one pound of rice, let it boil quite soft, then allow to cool. Stir in half a pound of flour, a spoonful of butter, two eggs. Make into dumplings with a spoon; boil in the soup in which a brisket of beef has been boiled. Can be eaten with meat, or served as a pudding with sugar and cinnamon. Time, half an hour to boil the rice, and twenty minutes the dumpling.

DUMPLINGS.—*See* Broodkluitjies.

E

EGGS — CURRIED
(Cape)

Ingredients:

1 oz. curry-powder	1 large onion, cut small, fried in butter
1 tbsp. vinegar	6 eggs
1 tsp. sugar	1 oz. butter
1 tsp. salt	
About ½ pint of rich stock	

Rub to a paste curry-powder, vinegar, sugar, etc. Mix with the stock; simmer this mixture well; break the eggs into it; let them simmer till done, like poached eggs. Serve quickly. Makes a nice breakfast or lunch dish. Time, about twenty minutes in all. *For four or five people.*

EGG FLIP
(Our own Recipe)

Ingredients:

1 bottle Madeira, or any light wine	Some cinnamon
1 pint water	A little nutmeg
5 eggs	12 cloves
1 tbsp. sugar	

Mull the wine, spices and sugar; add boiling water. Whisk in a punch-bowl the five eggs to a good froth. Pour in gradually the mulled wine, *steaming hot;* stir all the while. Put into tumblers and drink. Most excellent mixture for cold winter nights. This will make half a dozen tumblers.

EGGS — ITALIAN
(Mrs. Fleming's)

Hard-boiled eggs, cut in two, the yolks to be taken out, minced, and mixed with very finely minced cooked bacon, and some chopped parsley; put back into the whites arranged on a dish. Serve with mayonnaise dressing. *To be eaten cold.*

EGGS — POACHED

Eggs for poaching should be fresh, but not new-laid, or the white will not set. A stale egg will not poach. The best are about thirty-six hours old. Strain boiling water into a dry clean frying-pan. Break the egg into a cup, without damaging the yolk. When the water boils, gently slip the egg into it. Keep the water gently simmering till the white looks nicely set; take up gently with a slice. Serve on toasted bread, or slices of ham, or spinach. (In slipping the egg into the water keep the cup over it for half a minute, so as to gather the whites together.) In doing eggs in a frying-pan, never do more than four or five at a time. If liked, mix one tablespoonful of vinegar in the water in which you poach, one pint for an ordinary frying-pan. Time, two and a half, or three and a half minutes.

EGGS — SCRATCHED
(A favourite Colonial breakfast dish)

Take five or six eggs, whisk them well together; take a dessert-spoonful of butter in a frying-pan, let it get quite hot. Stir in the eggs; keep stirring briskly over the fire till done. Serve on hot buttered toast with pepper and salt.

EGGS — SNOW

Ingredients:

4 eggs	Sugar to taste
1 pint milk	Vanilla bean, or essence

Make a rich custard of the yolks; then whisk the whites. Flavour with vanilla and sweeten. Take a tablespoon at a time of the white froth and drop into boiling milk, turning carefully; then take it out and put it on a glass dish—go on till you have done all. Now pour the rich custard into the dish, not *over* the *snow*. *This makes a pretty, cool-looking supper dish.*

ENTRÉES — LUNCH AND SUPPER DISHES.—*See* Beef Olives, Croquettes, Eggs (Curried), Fritters (Beef, etc.), Gesmoorde Hoender, Patties (Lobster, etc.), Palates, Sasaties, Salsafy, Pudding (Roman), Ragout (Tongue), Swartsuur, Bredies, Bobotie, Calf's head Curries, Chicken and Poultry Dishes, Cutlets, Duck (Hashed), Irish Stew, Lamb (Stewed), Eggs (Curried), Fish Recipes, Hearts (Sheep), Heatherton, Veal Cake, Salad (Lobster), Macaroni Cheese, Marinade for Fish, Chops, Pancakes with Chicken, Pie (Fish, Macaroni, Pigeon, Steak, Veal and Kidney), Potato Curry Pie, Puddings (Cheese), Ragout of Cold Duck or Turkey, Ribs of Beef (Spiced, Cold), Rissoles (Meat and Fish), Salads (Fish), Sauce for Cold Boiled Fowl, Shape, Cold Meat, Steak (Pickled), Vegetables (Savoury), Vegetable Marrow (Stuffed), Risotto, Chestnut Chipolata, Haricot, Hash of Cold Beef, Fish Dishes.

F

FISH
(OLD DUTCH)

Put your fish (mackerel, or Cape "silverfish," or young "Kabel-jou,") in a tin baking-pan, with a good spoonful of butter; dredge with flour, pepper, and salt; add one tablespoonful chopped onion and some parsley, one blade of mace, one tablespoonful of anchovy essence, or two tablespoonfuls of tomato sauce, one cup of water. Put the pan in the oven, letting fish stew for twenty minutes, and serve. (Can be done in a baking-pot as well.) Is very nice for lunch or " high tea."

FISH — FOR BREAKFAST (D)
(MISS GAPPER'S)

Steep neat pieces of cold fish for an hour or two in a mixture of lemon-juice, salad-oil, pepper and salt. Then dip in batter and fry a rich brown in plenty of boiling lard (ox-marrow would do as well). Serve very hot.

FISH — BAKED
(HADDOCK IS BEST)

Ingredients :

1 oz. suet	A few leaves of thyme
1 oz. breadcrumbs	A little bit of bay leaf
1 tsp. chopped parsley	12 drops anchovy essence
½ tsp. Worcestershire sauce	

Mix all well together with one egg. well beaten; stuff the fish with it, sew it up. Butter the tin, then sprinkle in a little lemon juice. Score the fish to prevent it from shrinking. Put a spoonful of butter and some lemon-juice over the fish. Bake for twenty minutes and serve. *Very good.*

FISH BALLS
(MRS. FLEMING'S)

Take one small silver fish, crumb of one penny roll, a small piece of onion a little milk, one egg, parsley, pepper, and salt, put all through a mincing machine. Mix with the egg, the crumb to be soaked in milk and squeezed quite dry; roll in balls, dip in the bread-crumbs and egg. Fry in boiling lard or drippieg.

FISH — INGELEGDE, OR PICKLED
(CAPE WAY OF PRESERVING FISH)

Ingredients:

2 good-sized soles, or any nice Cape fish (filleted)	1 oz. mango relish
	6 large chillies, or 10 small
6 large onions	1 quart vinegar
2 oz. curry-powder	Salt to taste

Fry the fish a nice brown in lard, butter, or olive-oil; drain, and cool. Slice four onions, and fry a nice brown in a little oil; add one ounce curry-powder, two chillies cut fine, a dessertspoonful of salt, and the mango relish. When stirred to a paste, add a little vinegar to moisten well; then lay the fish in a jar; spread over each layer some of this mixture. Cut the rest of the onion in rings; boil in the vinegar very gently, until quite tender, with the other ounce of curry-powder and a little salt; then pour over the fish. Let it stand till cool, then cork well. It will be fit for use in two or three days, and will keep for months. *Is a delicious breakfast or lunch dish.*

ANOTHER RECIPE FOR INGELEGDE FISH

Substitute tumeric for curry-paste, and add the following ingredients to the onions, etc.: four or five red chillies, three dozen coriander seeds, half an ounce of ground ginger, a few lemon leaves, one ounce of sugar, one quart of good vinegar. Let these ingredients boil well. Then take the fillets of fish (which have been previously fried a nice brown colour in lard, and well drained), and put them carefully into the boiling mixture of curry, and just let it boil up. This ensures its keeping for months if well corked in small jars. At the Cape the best fish for pickling are " Kabeljou," " Geelbek," " Roman," etc.

FISH — FRIED

Cut your fish in nice little shapes; let them get slightly dry; dust with flour. Then roll in egg and bread-crumbs, with pepper and salt. Fry in lard. (In frying fish, do not add cold lard while your fish is in the frying-pan, as it should always be done in boiling fat or lard.

FISH AU GRATIN
(Miss Liesching's)

Clean and wash any medium-sized fish, such as pangar, harders or white stumpnose, put it in a shallow pan or enamelled dish, and cover with 2 oz. bread-crumbs, 2 oz. butter, some chopped onion and parsley, pepper and salt, all well mixed; put a little as stuffing for the fish, and sprinkle the remainder over. Put it in a hot oven for 20 minutes, and make the following sauce: The yolk of an egg, a dessert-spoonful of Harvey's sauce, and the same of Worcestershire (or tomato) sauce, a wineglassful of sherry and some cayenne pepper; mix all well together. Pour this sauce over the fish, and put it back into the oven for a few minutes. *Very good.*

FISH — LUNCHEON OR SUPPER DISH, HOT SNOEKPEKELAAR (D)
(Miss Breda's)

Snoekpekelaar is the name we give to fillets of snoek slightly salted and sun-dried. Take 2 fillets of snoekpekelaar, boil, pick out the bones while hot, on a hot dish, keeping it warm all the while. Have ready 6 large tomatoes, grilled. Mash up well, carefully removing the peel and any hard pieces. Add to this 1 tablespoon of vinegar, a little cayenne pepper, 1 oz. fresh butter, stirred to a cream, 1 tablespoon Lucca oil; sprinkle some salt over 2 white Spanish onions, cut up in thin slices, and pour boiling water on this to remove the roughness of the onion, leave for a few minutes, then drain. Now mix all the ingredients with the tomatoes.

Arrange the fish nicely. Heat the tomatoes, etc., and pour over the fish. Serve with boiled rice.

FISH MOULD
(Mrs. Fleming's)

Shred about half a pound, or more, of boiled fish; add half a cup of bread-crumbs, two eggs, essence of anchovy, two ounces of butter, pepper, salt, cayenne. Mix all well together, put into a buttered mould, and steam for an hour. Serve with butter sauce.

FISH — PENANG, OR FISH CURRY (D)
(Mrs. Cloete's)

Take 1 lb. of raw fish and cut it in fillets an inch or two square; of the fish-bones make about a pint of stock and strain, add one large onion cut in slices and browned in dripping or butter, one tablespoon of vinegar or lemon juice, one teaspoonful of sugar, one teaspoonful of salt, large tablespoonful of curry-powder. Mix all this well in the stock made of the fishbones, and let it come to the boil, now put the fillets of raw fish into this paste and cook for ten minutes, then serve with boiled rice. Boiled kreef can be similarly served, omitting the sugar.

FISH — PICKLED

Fry your fish, and brown in thin oil (an excellent alternative is Cape sheep-tail fat), *without flour or bread-crumbs*. Take two or three ounces of good curry-powder, two ounces soft sugar, two ounces salt, half-ounce pounded ginger, two or three fresh red chillies, two dozen coriander seeds, two quarts of vinegar, about four or five onions cut in rings and fried a nice brown. Boil all these ingredients. Lay your fish in layers in a jar, pour over each layer some of the mixture. Take care to have it well corked, and it will keep for months.

FISH PIE (D)

Ingredients:

Remains of cold fish	1 oz. butter
3 onions fried in dripping	Tomato sauce
Pepper	Mashed potatoes
Salt	Eggs
Mustard	

Break the fish in nice little pieces, mix well with onion, butter, seasoning, and some mashed potatoes. Slices of raw tomato in between are very nice. Pack the fish in a dish with a spoonful of butter or dripping at the bottom, then mash the potatoes with a little butter and pack on the top of the fish; brush over with an egg before baking. A few hard-boiled eggs mixed with the fish would be a great improvement, with some of the gravy in the fish-dish.

FISH SALAD — DUTCH HERRING (D)
(MRS. SPENCE'S)

Ingredients:

3 salted herrings	1 hard-boiled egg, the white chopped
1 large Spanish onion	and the yolk crumbled
1 tbsp. chopped parsley	

Soak the herrings in cold water for a night, then boil for 5 minutes and take out the bones. Pour boiling water over the sliced onion, which has been sprinkled with salt, to take off its roughness, drain it off and strain, mix the fish and onion together with some salad oil, pepper, and vinegar. Garnish the dish with chopped parsley, the egg, and beetroot cut in slices and stamped in pretty shapes, arranged in a pattern on the top of the salad. Penguin eggs, hard-boiled and sliced, may be added to the dish. A good supper dish.

FISH SAMBAL (D)
(MISS BREDA'S)

Pound some cold dry fish with some onion and red or green chillies, then add a spoonful of vinegar. Serve as a relish with bread-and-butter, or buttered toast.

FISH SCALLOP (D)

Break up some boiled fish into small pieces, have ready about the same proportion of fine breadcrumbs. Season the fish with pepper, salt, a dash of nutmeg, a spoonful of chopped parsley, and a few drops of anchovy sauce, and moisten with a little melted butter and some of the fish-jelly which collects in the dish in which the fish has stood. Butter some patty-pans and sprinkle with breadcrumbs. Put some fish-mixture in each, and cover with breadcrumbs. Put a pat of butter on the top of each; bake in a quick oven a light brown; lay the shells on a napkin on a hot dish and garnish with parsley.

FISH — SCALLOPED KREEF (D)

Ingredients:

3 lb. kreef.	1 tbsp. fine flour, and same of
½ pt. milk	chopped parsley
A little blade of mace boiled in the	½ cup stale bread-crumbs
milk	½ tsp. or less cayenne
2 oz. butter	1 tsp. salt

Let the milk boil, rub the flour and butter together and stir into the boiling milk, let it boil up nice and smooth for a sauce. Boil the lobster, open and cut the meat into dice-shaped pieces. Put a layer of white sauce at the bottom of the baking-dish—then a layer of lobster seasoned with salt and cayenne, and a sprinkling of parsley and bread-crumbs, adding sauce and lobster alternately till the dish is filled; the *last* layer should be white sauce, sprinkled with bread-crumbs and a little melted butter on the top.

Put in a quick oven to brown and get thoroughly warm. It can be replaced in the shell to be served—or left in the pie-dish, the outside of which should be garnished with frilled papers.

FISH — SMOORVIS (D)
(OUR OWN RECIPE)

The dried fish is first parboiled and then, with two forks, broken up into pieces, all bones being carefully taken out. Meanwhile cut up an onion and fry it a light-brown in dripping in a flat pot, and slice up a few potatoes, boiled or raw, and a red chilli (or if that is too hot add a little pinch of cayenne); a cupful of any stock (this may be mutton or made of fish-bones) is added to the mixture, then the pieces of fish are put in and all simmered for an hour. Smoorvis, an old Malay speciality, is an excellent dish for luncheon. Tomatoes, if in season, may be added to it.

FISH — SOUSED, A LUNCHEON DISH
(MRS. CLOETE OF ALPHEN. A COLD LUNCHEON OR BREAKFAST DISH.)

Ingredients:

Remains of cold, boiled, fish	A few allspice (whole)
1 oz. of Lucca oil	A cut up red chilli
A large onion sliced	A few bay leaves, if liked, or a few
2 oz. vinegar	coriander seeds

Cut the onion very thinly and pour a little salt and boiling water over it; then drain, and lay the fish in a pie-dish with onion, spices, oil, vinegar, in layers. Let it stand for an hour or more. Then cover over and steam in a cool oven for a quarter of an hour. To be eaten cold.

FISH — STEWED
(MRS. FLEMING'S BOOK)

Fillet your fish, and fry in lard (bread-crumb and egg); slice an onion, and fry that also. Then put the fish and onion in a tin dish and cover with fish stock; season with pepper and salt, one blade of mace, a clove or two, a few balls of butter (rolled in flour) to thicken the gravy, two tablespoons ketchup. Leave in the oven an hour or two, with the lid on the tin. Serve with little rissoles made from the trimmings fried in lard. *Very good.*

FISH IN WHITE SAUCE (D)
(MISS LE SUEUR'S)

For the white sauce, rub an oz. or two of butter in 2 tablespoonfuls flour, add to it a few spoonfuls of stock made of the fish-bones boiled with an onion till the latter is nice and tender; and then take half a cupful of milk and pour it over. Flavour with lemon, cayenne, chopped parsley, pepper and salt. Cut up the fish, which must be raw, into neat pieces sufficient for a helping, and let it simmer in the mixture for a few minutes.

FISH.—*See* Luncheon Dish, Kedgeree, Oysters, Fish Pie, Perlemoen, and Kreef. *See also* Sauces for Fish, Marinade (German).

FLAVOURING MIXTURE

Ingredients:

½ oz. nutmeg
½ oz. mace
1 oz. white pepper

1 oz. cloves
½ oz. each of thyme, marjoram, basil
¼ oz. bay leaves

Thoroughly dry all, and pound fine. *Cork well.* Useful in force-meats, pies, soups, etc.

FORCEMEAT OR STUFFING
(MRS. ETHERIDGE'S)

A little parsley (cut fine), three ounces of beef suet, some pepper, salt, lemon-peel, bread-crumbs, one egg. Moisten, if necessary, with a little milk. If to be eaten cold, use butter instead of beef suet.

FOWLS.—*See also* Chicken and Gesmoorde Hoender, Indian Pilau, Heatherton.

FOWL — BOILED

After the fowl is nicely stuffed and trussed, tie it into a floured cloth, put into a stewing-pan, cover with hot water, let it simmer very gently for an hour and a half; put it on a hot dish, and pour over it a white sauce or a little chopped parsley and butter. Serve with tongue or ham. Garnish the dish with nicely grilled bacon. (Take care the water boils *before* the fowl is put in.)

FOWL — FRICASSEED

Ingredients:

The remains of cold roast fowl
1 strip of lemon peel
1 blade of pounded mace
1 bunch of savoury herbs
1 onion

Pepper and salt
1 pint water
1 tsp. of flour
¼ pint of cream
The yolks of 2 eggs

Divide the remains of fowl into nice little joints; make gravy of the trimmings and legs by stewing them with lemon-peel, mace, herbs, onion, seasoning, and water, until reduced to half a pint; when strained, put in fowl. Warm through and through, thicken with a teaspoonful of flour; stir the yolks of eggs into the cream and add. Let it get thoroughly hot, but *do not boil*. Time, one hour to make the gravy, a quarter of an hour to warm the fowl.

FOWL — ROAST
(THE OLD CAPE WAY, IN A BAKING-POT)

Ingredients:

2 young fowls killed the day before	A glass of wine
A few slices of bacon	1 oz. of butter and fat
Pepper and salt	

After having carefully picked, and singed the small feathers by burning a clean paper over the fowl, cut off the neck and skewer the skin down over the back. Cut off the claws, dip the legs in boiling water, scrape them, and turn the pinions under; run a skewer through them and the middle of the leg through the body, to the pinion and leg on the other side. The liver and gizzard should be placed in the wings, the liver on one side, the gizzard on the other. Tie the legs by passing a trussing-needle, threaded with twine, through the backbone, and securing on the other side. Now place your chickens, with the breast down, in a baking-pot; if not quite young and tender put half a pint of water in a baking-pot, also a little of the butter and fat. In an hour's time turn the chickens over, put over them some more butter and fat, and a glass of wine. Put on the outside of the lid of the baking-pot some coals of wood fire. When the chickens are nice and brown, send them in. Garnish with some fried bacon, and serve with bread sauce. Time, about one hour and a half.

FOWL SAUTÉ — WITH GREEN PEAS OR MUSHROOMS
(AN ENTRÉE)

Ingredients:

The remains of cold roast chicken	1 dessertsp. of flour
1 oz. butter	½ pint of weak stock
A saltsp. of pepper	1 pint of green peas
Salt	1 tsp. of sugar
A little nutmeg	

Cut up the fowl into nice pieces, put it into a stewing-pan with the butter, let it fry a nice brown, having sprinkled it with pepper and salt. Dredge in the flour, shake the ingredients well about, then add the stock and peas. Stew till the latter are tender, which will be twenty minutes. Arrange the chicken round and the peas in the middle. Mushrooms may be substituted for peas.

FOWLS — STEWED
(MY MOTHER'S. THE CAPE WAY OF COOKING A PAIR OF YOUNG FOWLS)

Ingredients:

2 nice young fowls	A tbsp. of butter and one of fat
2 onions	A wineglass of white wine
A blade of mace	2 oz. of vermicelli
1 doz. allspice and 12 peppercorns	1 oz. macaroni
put in a tiny muslin bag	Stuffing for the chicken

Have your chickens nicely cleaned and singed. Set them on a slow fire in a flat baking-pot with a cup of water, two or three white onions (only peeled and slit across the top), the little bag of spice, and the butter and fat. Let it simmer for an hour (the chickens to be skewered and stuffed with the ordinary stuffing used for turkey, etc.), turning the breast downwards. When nearly done, stir in the vermicelli and macaroni. Add a little *white* stock if necessary. Remove the bag of spice and place the fowls on a dish, and just before serving whip up an egg with a glass of wine or some lemon juice, and pour over the chickens. Serve. *Very good.*

FRIKKADELS — OR SAVOURY RISSOLES
(Dutch)

Ingredients:

Some minced mutton (raw is nicer than cooked), seasoned well with pepper, salt and nutmeg

A *suspicion* of onion

For 1 lb. meat—1 quarter of a nutmeg, ½ tsp. pepper and salt
A slice or two of white bread soaked in milk
A tbsp. tomato sauce
1 egg

For 1 lb. meat — a quarter of a nutmeg, half a teaspoon pepper and salt.

Mix all well together, roll in round shapes, put in egg and breadcrumbs, fry in hot fat. Stewed in a rich *curry-sauce*, this is a nice entrée.

FRIKKADELS
(Cape)

First stew the Frikkadels in a rich stock, in which a slice of browned onion has been put; when nearly done, add the mushrooms, and let them stew gently, with a good lump of butter. *With mushrooms they are most delicious.*

FRIED BREAD
(A homely dish)

Take slices of brown bread, fry them a nice brown with some dripping (either mutton, beef, or chicken); serve warm with pepper. *Very nice for breakfast.*

FRITTERS — BEEF

Ingredients:

Some cold roast beef
10 oz. flour
2 oz. butter
A cupful of water

Whites of 2 eggs
Salt, pepper, and a scraping of nutmeg

Mix to a smooth batter the flour, with water or milk; melt the butter, stir into the flour with the whites of two eggs, whisked. Shred the beef as thin as possible, season to your taste, and add it to the batter; mix all well together, and drop with a spoon into boiling dripping or lard. Drain well from the fat. Serve hot.

FRITTERS — BEEF
(ANOTHER MODE)

Take slices from the undercut of sirloin; flavour your batter with a seasoning of pepper, pounded allspice, and salt, dip the slices of beef in it, and fry in boiling lard a nice brown. Take care the meat is well covered with batter.

FRITTERS — INDIAN

Ingredients:

3 tbsps. of flour	The whites of 2 eggs
The yolk of 4 eggs	Hot lard, or clarified dripping

Put the flour in a basin, and mix it with enough boiling water to make a stiff paste; stir all the time, to prevent its getting lumpy. Let it cool a little, then break into it the yolks of four eggs and the whites of two; stir all well together. Have ready some boiling lard or clarified dripping; drop a dessertspoonful of batter at a time, and fry the fritters a light brown. They should rise like balls. Time, five or eight minutes to fry. *Sufficient for four or five people.*

FRITTERS — ANOTHER WAY
(A VERY CHEAP CAPE RECIPE)

Ingredients:

1½ cupfuls of flour	Ginger
Skim milk	½ tsp. carbonate of soda

Mix well with the flour a pinch of salt, half a teaspoonful of carbonate of soda, a little pounded ginger, about a cupful of thick milk; mix into a nice smooth paste. Have ready some boiling lard or clarified dripping, and drop in the paste; each small spoonful will rise into a ball. Serve hot, with sugar and lemon.

FRITTERS — ORANGE

Mix with eight ounces of flour two ounces of butter, then add one pint of water, then the whites of two eggs, to make a batter. Peel three oranges, cut across, and take out the seeds, cut in slices, dip each slice into the thick batter, fry, serve with sugar.

Slices of cold plum-pudding fried in batter in this way make delicious fritters.

FRITTERS — PINEAPPLE (D)

Pare and core a pineapple; cut it into slices and stew them with a little water, sugar, and lemon-peel. When soft, add a little white wine and the juice of half a lime, with a pat of butter.

When cold, make a batter of 3 spoonfuls of fine flour, 2 spoons of cream, a glass of white wine, some sugar, and four eggs. Beat it all well together. Put a little butter in a frying-pan, drop the fruit into the batter you have made, and taking it out in spoonfuls, fry them one by one in the butter to a nice light-brown. Put them on a sieve before the fire to dry, and serve hot, with plenty of pounded sugar over them on a white napkin.

FRITTERS — POTATO
(BESSIE'S)

Ingredients:

6 large mealy potatoes (mashed)	2 eggs
1 tbsp. of fine flour	A little salt
1 tbsp. of butter, or cream	1 tsp. of cinnamon

Mix all well together, make in little flat cakes, fry in boiling lard or clarified dripping. Serve with sugar and cinnamon.

A similar recipe for sweet potatoes, half a pound of which will be required (boiled and mashed), and two spoonfuls of cream, instead of one. If eggs are scarce, use half a teaspoonful of carbonate of soda, instead of the two eggs.

FRITTERS — PUMPKIN

Stew a sweet pumpkin; when soft, add a few ounces of flour to thicken it. For two cups of pumpkin take a good slice of white bread soaked in milk and squeezed *very dry*. Mix well together with a pinch of salt, some cinnamon, and a quarter of a teaspoonful of carbonate of soda and two eggs. Fry in boiling fat. Serve hot, with sugar and cinnamon.

FRUIT — BOTTLED
(MRS. ROSE INNES'S)

Ingredients:

1 gill of water	Mason's jars (with screw tops)
1 gill of sugar to every lb. of fruit	

Take the proportions of sugar and water, and boil. When boiling, put in the *fresh, ripe fruit* you intend bottling; let it boil till tender, and bottle at once. The jars must be *hot*, and filled to overflowing, and *closed at once*. Have your bottles in a saucepan on the stove, side by side with the fruit you are preparing, so as to ensure their being hot when the fruit is ready. Lay the jars on a little straw in the saucepan, *in cold water*, and allow the water to boil. Place the jars on soup-plates (as they are to overflow), so that the syrup is not wasted. Fruit done this way will keep over two years.

The moment apricots and plums boil up they are ready; also mulberries and gooseberries; but peaches, apples, quinces and guavas, require a longer time.

The bottled fruit is very good eaten with cream, when a little more sugar may be added if wanted.

G

GESMOORDE HOENDER — AN OLD FASHIONED ENTRÉE
(MALAY, MRS. D. CLOETE'S)

Ingredients:

A young fowl	White pepper, salt
2 large white onions	*A green chilli*
A little nutmeg	2 oz. butter

Fry your onions a golden brown in some butter or fat. Then cut the chicken in nice little joints, let them brown in a little butter. It must be done quickly, *take care not to burn.* Then add the onion, an *idea* of nutmeg, some pepper, half a cup of water; let it simmer for an hour. Just before dishing add a *green chilli* cut up. Toss it about well. The chilli gives a most delicate flavour. Should the chicken look dry, add a little stock. *Enough for six people. Very good.*

GINGER BEER
(MRS. J. CLOETE'S)

Ingredients:

5 lb. sugar	½ a bucket of boiled water
1 lb. ginger, bruised	

Put into a small cask, let it draw for a day, then fill with cold water, a bottle of yeast, two packets of cream of tartar. Two days after, it may be bottled. If yeast is not to be had, add two bottles of beer instead.

GINGER BEER — ANOTHER

Ingredients:

8 lemons	1 bottle brandy
3 lb. sugar	1 cup pounded ginger
3 tbsps. cream of tartar	

Mix all well together, pour into a small cask, fill with water. Leave for two days, shaking well; bottle the third.

GINGER POP
(ADMIRAL ETHERIDGE'S)

Ingredients:

2 lb. of lump sugar	2 gallons of boiling water
2 lemons (juice and peel)	1 oz. cream of tartar
2 oz. best ginger, cut or bruised	

Mix, and when cool add a tablespoonful of yeast on toast. Let it stand for twelve hours. Strain through a coarse cloth and bottle, tying the corks down. The white of one egg well beaten, and added just before corking, is a great improvement for using soon. *Three days will do.*

GINGERBREAD — TALKE O' THE HILL,
GINGERBREAD LOAF

Put ¼ lb. butter into 1 lb. flour, add ¼ lb. coarse sugar, ¼ oz. baking-powder, 1 oz. caraway seeds, 2 oz. ground ginger, 2 oz. candied peel, cut small, ¼ lb. raisins chopped, 2 eggs, a wineglassful of sherry, 1 lb. treacle, warmed; mix all well together and bake 3 hours in a slow oven. Allow plenty of room in the tin for rising, and if the cake begins to brown too soon, cover it with paper.

GLAZE (D)

To make clear dark-brown glaze, which so much improves the look of cold pressed beef or tongue, you must have ordinary good gravy, and by constant boiling reduce to, say, a quarter the original quantity, which when cold will jelly. You can make it as thick a glaze as you like by successive coats being brushed over the meat, but be sure the under one is dry before applying the next.

GRAPES IN BRANDY
(MRS. CLOETE'S)

Take nice ripe Hanepoot grapes, cut them with a piece of the stalk prick with a steel pin; fill a jar. Then take VERY thick syrup, previously boiled, two cups of syrup to one of good spirits of wine. Fill the jars, cover well; tie down with bladder.

GRAPE JAM
(HOME RECIPE)

Ingredients:
4 lb. fruit   2 lb. sugar

Carefully pick the grapes from the bunches, prick with a steel pin. Boil a syrup of the sugar, put the grapes into the boiling syrup. Some sliced apple or quince may be added to the grapes, for every pound of quince one of sugar, some cut-up orange peel. Boil rather quickly at first. Take some of the preserve and lay it on a saucer to cool to see if it is ready; if so it will jelly.

Another very nice way of making grape jam is to take the Hanepoot grape before it is quite sweet and ripe, then take equal parts of sugar and fruit, pick from the bunches, and put into a preserving-pan with a few cups of water, and allow the grapes to stew for half an hour. Skim off all the grape seeds, add the sugar (and if you like, a few pounds of stewing apples), let all boil briskly, stirring *constantly* with a wooden spoon. If done in small quantities (not more than six pounds) it does not take more than two hours, and becomes quite like a jelly when done.

61

B

GRATED CHEESE AND CAULIFLOWER
(CHOUXFLEURS AU GRATIN. MISS LIESCHING'S)

Ingredients:

A fine head of cauliflower	The yolk of an egg
4 tbsps. of cream or milk	2 oz. of fine bread-crumbs
A few slices of onion, chopped fine	1 saltsp. of salt
2 oz. of mild cheese, grated	½ saltsp. of pepper and cayenne

Boil the milk with the chopped onion, then add the grated cheese (keeping a little for sprinkling afterwards), let it boil up; draw it aside and add gradually the yolk of the egg, pepper, salt, cayenne, and bread-crumbs. Mix all thoroughly, keep nice and warm, and pour over the cauliflower, which should be ready (having been previously boiled nice and tender in a saucepan of water with the head downwards, leaving the pot open); break the cauliflower into neat little pieces (remove all green and stalk), pour the mixture over the cauliflower on a baking-dish, and then on top a little more bread-crumbs and grated cheese. Bake for a few minutes in the oven, and serve with cutlets.

Vegetable Marrows done in this way are very good.

GRAVY — A NICE (D)

This is a good gravy for mutton, beef, game, or poultry. When the roast is done, remove some of the fat from the brown sauce in the baking-dish, add a cup of thick cream (or half a cup of milk with a teaspoon of maizena stirred into it), mix it with the brown gravy, put into the baking-pan with a spoonful of dripping; stir all well over a quick fire to brown, *but not burn.*

H

HAMS — HOW TO CURE THEM
(PROVED BY LONG EXPERIENCE TO BE AN EXCELLENT RECIPE)

After cutting the hams, rough-salt them for a night, letting all the water drain away.

For a ham weighing twelve or fourteen pounds take as follows: two pounds of salt, one pound *brownest* sugar, two ounces saltpetre, four ounces black pepper, four ounces allspice, and a handful of coriander seeds. Bruise the spices and saltpetre, mix all well with the salt, and have the ham rubbed well with the hand and a little flat stone for half an hour every day for three days, till the skin feels soft, and the salt, etc., looks like a creamy substance. In rubbing divide the salt, sugar, etc., into portions, and take a fresh portion every time, taking care to turn the ham skin downwards, and cover with the salt, etc. When all has been used, and the ham rubbed three days, take *all* the brine that has formed and boil it with two pints of vinegar and two pints of good ale. Skim it well, and when cool pour over the ham, leaving it in this pickle for a month. Then dry it, put under a press, brush with a little tar mixed with treacle and some bran. Smoke for three weeks, and hang in a cool, dry place.

The above pickle does beautifully for sides of bacon, or any other pork that has to be smoked.

When wanted for use, before boiling, soak the ham for a night, simmer gently for three or four hours. Let your water *boil* before putting in the ham, and *then gently simmer.*

HAM — TO USE UP COLD HAM (D)

Take pieces of both fat and lean and pound in a mortar (or pass through a minching-machine), add to that 1 slice of white bread boiled in half a pint of milk and 1 egg well beaten, mix all and bake in a mould.

HAM — POTTED, TO USE UP COLD A HAM (D)
(Miss Gapper's)

Take any remains of ham, trim off all the dry pieces and pass the rest through a mincing-machine, adding pepper and a dash of nutmeg (grated) and pound all well in a mortar; pack tightly into small pots and pour melted butter over the top. If you have any cold chicken at the same time it can be added to the ham. Corned beef or tongue may be potted in the same way. (Very nice for picnic sandwiches.)

HAM TOAST
(Breakfast Dish)

Chop up some lean ham, put into a pan with a lump of butter, a little pepper, and two well-beaten eggs. When well warmed spread on hot buttered toast. Serve.

Another similar breakfast dish is as follows:

Put into a stewpan three tablespoonfuls of cream or milk, some grated tongue, beef, pepper, and salt. When hot put in four eggs, well beaten; stir all the time till the mixture is thick. Have some buttered toast, spread the mixture on, and send to table very hot.

HAM.—*See* Omelette (Ham).

HARDERS.—*See* Herrings.

HARE — JUGGED

Ingredients:

1 hare	½ tsp. of black pepper
A few sweet herbs	A strip of lemon-peel
2 onions	Thickening of butter and flour
4 cloves	2 tbsps. of mushroom ketchup
6 whole allspice	½ pint of port or other dark wine

Skin and wash the hare nicely; cut it up into joints, not too large; dredge with flour, and fry in butter a nice brown; then put into a stewing-pan with the herbs, onions, cloves, allspice, pepper, and lemon-peel; cover with hot water, and when it boils carefully remove the scum, and let it simmer gently till tender (which will be in about one hour and three-quarters if the hare is old). Then take out the pieces of hare, thicken the gravy with flour and butter add the ketchup and port wine, let it boil ten minutes; strain through a sieve on the pieces of hare. Let it simmer for two minutes so as to be nice and warm. A few forcemeat balls (*see* Forcemeat Recipe) stewed in the gravy ten minutes before dishing, is an improvement. Serve with quince or red currant jelly.

HARICOT
(Cape name, Hutspot)

Ingredients:

4 lb. of shoulder, or best end of neck of mutton	4 carrots
1 onion	Some sugar loaf cabbage
3 or 4 potatoes	About a cup of green peas
	Some salt and cayenne pepper

Put the mutton in a flat stewing-pot, let it fry a pale brown (but do not cook enough for eating), with the onion cut in slices; then cover the pot, and let it stew gently with the other ingredients for two or three hours. *This is a delicious dish.*

HASH OF COLD MUTTON OR BEEF
(A cheap gravy for hashes, etc.)

Ingredients:

Bones and trimmings of a cold joint intended for hashing	1 fried onion
¼ tsp. of salt	1 carrot
¼ tsp. of whole pepper	1 oz. butter
¼ tsp. of allspice	Flour, for thickening
Some savoury herbs	Sufficient water to cover the bones well

Chop the bones very fine; put into a stewing-pan with the salt, pepper, spices; cover with boiling water. Let the whole simmer gently for two hours. Slice and fry onions till a pale brown, and mix with gravy made from the bones; boil a little while, strain and put back into the saucepan. Thicken with a little flour rubbed in butter, or a little plain *browned* flour, a pinch of brown sugar, and some tomato sauce. Let it all boil well. Lastly put in your nicely cut up meat, taking care that it never boils, or it immediately becomes *hard*. Serve with toast round the dish, or fried sippets. A little cayenne pepper is nice in hashes. Time for gravy, about two or three hours.

HEARTS — SHEEP'S (D)
(A COUNTRY LUNCHEON DISH. MRS. FAURE'S)

Wash the hearts well in hot water, then dip them in cold to whiten them (just as one would do sheep's brains). Then make a well-mixed stuffing of a small cupful of bread-crumbs, and the same amount of chopped suet, one tablespoonful of finely-chopped onion, and flavoured with thyme, sage, pepper and salt. With this fill the cavities of the hearts and skewer together. Simmer them in water just covering the hearts, till quite tender, for about an hour and a half, then braise or fry them with a little butter. Serve cut in slices, with a nice brown gravy to which has been added a little tomato sauce.

HEATHERTON
(OR FRIAR'S CHICKEN)

One pint of water, one ounce of butter—let this boil. Cut up a chicken, stew it in the liquor for an hour. Take the chicken out of the stock, and keep warm in a hot dish. Flavour the stock with a dash of nutmeg, some white pepper, a blade of mace, and a little lemon; let it boil up. Remove from the fire. Whisk up two or three eggs, stir into the mixture (after removing the mace) as you would custard, let it thicken, *but not boil*, pour over the chicken, etc., and serve hot.

Fish, or any tender veal or lamb, may be done this way.

HERRINGS — CAPE HARDERS
(MRS. FLEMING'S)

Roast on a gridiron; serve with a little butter, chopped parsley, vinegar, or lemon-juice. *Very good.*

Harders soaked in water for a night, and broiled in a buttered paper on a gridiron, are very good.

The small dried and salted herring commonly called at the Cape " Bokkom," is very good when done this way: pour boiling water on it, and then steam in a covered pan with a little fat. When tender, remove the skins, and serve hot.

HEUNINGKOEK OR HONEY CAKE

Ingredients:

6 lb. of flour   1½ quart bottles of honey
2 lb. sugar

Boil sugar and honey together; add one dessertspoonful cloves, two dessertspoonfuls cinnamon, ground, remove from the fire. Add the weight of the egg in potash, and one wineglass of brandy. Mix the flour with two teaspoonfuls of soda; then mix the hot syrup and flour well together, working the dough well with the hands; roll out thinly. Put in a buttered pan and bake in a slow oven for an hour. Cut into squares. Preserved citron, cut into strips and mixed with the dough, improves the flavour. One-quarter of this quantity is enough for a small family. Will keep for some time.

I

ICE.—*See* Cream (Chocolate), Iced.

ICING FOR CAKES
(MRS. D. CLOETE'S)

Ingredients:

1 lb. icing sugar   Whites of 3 eggs

Whisk the eggs to a stiff froth and gradually sift in the sugar. Beat the mixture well, until the sugar is smooth; then with a broad knife lay the icing equally over the cake, laying on one layer first and allowing it to get firm in a cool oven before you put on the next layer, and so on. The icing may be coloured with a little cochineal or currant juice. Spinach juice gives a nice *green* colour. For a sponge-cake the icing may be flavoured with orange or vanilla. Dry the icing in a cool oven before sending to the table.

For ornamental icing put layer of white sugar icing first, then mix a little cochineal with some icing. Make a kind of cornucopia of paper, leaving a small hole at the bottom; fill with the red icing and press it out through the hole, when it can be guided into patterns or raised into dots, etc. Ornamental squeezers can be obtained at ironmongers for this purpose. For a sponge-cake flavoured with orange, it makes a nice change to put a layer of marmalade over the cake, and the icing, also flavoured with orange, over that.

ICING FOR CAKES — ALMOND

Ingredients:

1 lb. almonds   Whites of 2 eggs
¾ lb. finely pounded loaf sugar

Blanch the almonds and pound them in a mortar, adding a little cold water or white of egg during the pounding to keep the almonds from oiling. Whisk the whites of the two eggs to a stiff froth, mix with the almonds, beat well together to a smooth paste. Ice the cake with a broad knife, adding layer upon layer, allowing it to dry in between.

ICING FOR CAKES — CHOCOLATE (D)
(MISS MAY VAN RENEN'S)

Put ¼ lb. grated chocolate with 3 tablespoons of cold water in an enamelled saucepan; boil for 5 minutes, then stir in 6 oz. icing-sugar. Let it just come to the boil; take off the fire, stir well, and spread over any cake you wish to ice quickly. Sponge-cake and this icing in layers and the icing also over all would be excellent.

ICING FOR CAKES — COFFEE (D)

Work together 5 oz. of icing sugar with 2 oz. of fresh butter; to this add 1½ tablespoonfuls of essence of coffee, or coffee made very strong; let it cool before adding to the butter and sugar. Spread evenly on the cake.

ICING FOR CAKES (D)
(MRS. GRIFFITHS'S)

Two large cups of fine white sugar, with just enough hot water to melt it; set it to boil in an earthenware saucepan, stirring occasionally till it threads from the spoon. Beat the whites of two eggs to a stiff froth, put in a deep basin, and pour the boiling sugar over the stiffly beaten whites, beating all the time.

ICING FOR CAKES — VANILLA

Take 1 large cupful of white sugar, and put it in a clean enamelled saucepan, with just as much boiling water as will melt the sugar, adding this little by little. Stir over the fire and let it boil till it threads off the spoon. Beat the white of 1 egg, flavour when well whisked with half a teaspoonful of vanilla or lemon, and put in a round basin, over which pour the boiling syrup—beating all the time. When nearly cold, use to ice.

ICE COCOANUT

Ingredients:

    1 cocoanut grated   Milk of the cocoanut
    1¼ lb. white sugar

First put the sugar in an enamelled saucepan on the fire, with two tablespoons of the milk. When the sugar is dissolved, add the cocoanut and boil ten minutes. Take care it does not burn. Oil a tin well, and pour in the mixture, colouring half with cochineal. Leave in mould till cold. (*See* Cocoanut Ice).

ICE CREAM — GINGER
(Mrs. Southey's)

Make a custard with half a pint of milk, the yolks of two eggs, and three ounces of sugar; add half a pint of whipped cream and some preserved ginger, cut in small pieces, and freeze. If cream is not procurable, make a little more custard with the yolks of four eggs. Whip the whites to a stiff froth and mix with the custard while hot. Add the preserved ginger when the custard has cooled, and freeze.

ICE CREAM — VANILLA
(Mrs. Southey's)

Make a custard with three eggs and half a pint of milk, sweetened with three ounces of sugar. Whip half a pint of cream and mix with custard. Flavour with essence of vanilla, and freeze.

ICE — STRAWBERRY WATER

Crush some ripe strawberries and strain a pint of juice; sweeten with clarified sugar, and freeze.

INDIAN PILAU
(Miss Liesching's)

Ingredients:

3 oz. of butter	A tiny piece of cinnamon
4 cloves	12 Peppercorns
4 cardomom seeds	¾ lb. of white rice
2 hard-boiled eggs	A young fowl
Bacon	A pint of good stock or gravy
3 onions	(Put all the spices into a muslin bag)

Slice the onions very fine, fry a nice brown in the butter, then add the stock, the rice, *well washed*, and a few slices of bacon or corned pork. Put all into a flat saucepan and cover with one pint of water, taking care to have two inches of gravy above the rice. When the rice is *all but done*, have ready a boiled fowl, nicely trussed, lay it in the middle of the rice, cover the pot and let it simmer till the rice is nice and dry; serve with the rice all round the fowl, garnished with hard-boiled egg and slices of bacon. Take care to remove the bag of spices. Shoulder of mutton or lamb may be done the same way, the only difference being that the meat should be put in raw with the rice, and no stock need be added.

INVALID COOKERY

BARLEY WATER

Take half a cup of pearl barley, wash well, and boil in the same way as the recipe for a pleasant gruel; but will require a longer time —one hour. Sweeten to taste, and add orange and lemon.

BEEF TEA

Cut up the meat in small pieces, putting in a jar till the juice is extracted. The jar to be corked and kept in a saucepan of boiling water for two hours. A little isinglass increases the nourishment. A teaspoonful at a time.

BEEF TEA — ANOTHER

Take an ounce of raw beef, from the shin or rump (freshly killed). Mince very fine, put into a cup with a tablespoonful of cold water, let it stand for a quarter of an hour, strain, and give a teaspoonful at a time.

BEEF TEA — VERY STRONG

Mince two pounds of lean beef or mutton, put it into a jar without water (closely covered), stand it in an oven for an hour and a half till every drop of gravy is out of the meat. Mix this rich stock with boiling water to the proper strength required.

BILTONG.— *See* Biltong Recipe, earlier in the book ; is both appetising and nourishing for invalids.

CHICKEN BROTH — H. D.

Take an old fowl; cut very small; set on the fire with two quarts of cold water, a few peppercorns, allspice, and salt. Let it boil *slowly*, in a *closed* pot, till the chicken is in shreds. Strain; may be thickened with a little vermicelli, if liked. Will take four hours. The yolk of an egg, whipped up with a little lemon-juice, stirred into the broth just before serving, is both nourishing and appetising.

MUTTON BROTH

Ingredients:

2 lb. of scrag-end, or neck of mutton	1 tbsp. pearl barley
2 quarts of water	A carrot, or turnip

Boil all well together for three hours or more; strain thoroughly with a kitchen strainer. The neck of mutton makes a more tasty broth than the same quantity of beef.

CHICKEN CREAM OR MINCE

Take a nice young fowl; boil it in a cloth. When done, take the breast and upper part of the leg; mince and pound in a mortar. Chop up the rest of the chicken, with all the bones broken; put in a stewpan with a quart of water, a few allspice, a little nutmeg and pepper; let it stew to a pint or less; rub the minced chicken through a sieve into this gravy, after it has been strained. Thicken with two spoonfuls of good fresh cream, or a little maizena, rubbed in a pat of butter— not too rich. This mixture can be heated in a mug in a saucepan of boiling water. Don't forget a little salt. Two or three spoonfuls may be taken by an invalid.

A MUTTON CHOP
(FROM THE UNDERCUT)

Take a slice from the undercut of a saddle of mutton, sprinkle with pepper, and grill on a very hot gridiron, turning frequently. Don't put a fork into it. When done rub a little bit of fresh butter on it, and some salt. It will be found delicate and tasty. Serve very hot. The chop may also be cut out of the middle of a leg of mutton.

CUSTARD PUDDING

Few invalids ever tire of the plain, old-fashioned custard made in this way: Two eggs, well whipped, mixed with one pint of milk and a spoonful of sugar; bake in an oven, standing the basin in a dish with water in it to prevent burning.

The Schaum pudding (*see* Puddings) is another favourite.

EGG AND SHERRY

Whisk up the white of an egg to a stiff froth; take a wineglass of sherry and a little sugar; whisk all up well. *Both nourishing and pleasant.*

EGG SILKY

Whisk the yolk, or the whole egg, very well; grate a little nutmeg on it; take a good teaspoonful of sugar, stir well together; pour in gradually about half a tumbler of boiling water; lastly, add a wine-glass of whisky. *This is an excellent mixture for a cold.*

A PLEASANT GRUEL

Take a small cup of good *wheaten* bran, mix with a little cold water, then stir in two quarts of boiling water, into which a stick of cinnamon has been put; let it boil for half an hour, till sufficiently thick; strain, and when to be taken add a teaspoonful of lemon or orange and as much sugar as you like. *Good for colds.*

STRENGTHENING JELLY

Ingredients:

1 pint of port wine	1 oz. gum arabic
2 oz. isinglass	½ a nutmeg grated
2 oz. white wine	Sugar to taste

Put these ingredients in a jar, tie it over ; put the jar into a saucepan till all is dissolved; it must be stirred constantly. When cold it will be a firm jelly. Give the invalid a piece the size of a nutmeg at a time.

A WINE JELLY FOR INVALIDS

Take the juice of two oranges, and the peel of one, the yolks of four eggs, an ounce of isinglass (or a stiff jelly, procured from calves' feet or sheep's trotters, about one pint), half a pint of sherry or white wine, one wineglass of good cognac, ten cloves, a little cinnamon, and two tablespoonfuls of sugar. Stir all well together, put into a stewpan. When it boils up draw it aside for five minutes; pour in two tablespoonfuls of cold water. Strain through a jelly-bag. Use *good* sherry, and freshly laid eggs.

SOUP FOR INVALIDS
((Dr. Versfeld's)

Take two pounds of good lean mutton or beef. Pass twice through a mincing-machine so that every particle is well mashed. Set it on the fire with two quarts of water. Let it boil slowly for three hours or more, so that it is reduced to one quart or less. Add salt, and any flavouring that is liked; a few peppercorns and allspice. Strain through a gravy strainer before serving.

Boil two knuckles of veal in three quarts of milk till reduced to a half. Flavour with a little mace or nutmeg, salt to be added when done. Half this quantity does at a time.

IRISH STEW

Ingredients:

3 lb. loin or neck of mutton	Pepper, salt
5 lb. potatoes	Rather more than one pint of water
3 onions	

Cut the mutton into chops of moderate thickness, pare and slice the potatoes, and cut the onions in rings. Put a layer of potatoes at the bottom of the stewing-pan, then a layer of mutton and onions; season with pepper and salt. Proceed in this manner till all is used. Take care to have plenty of vegetables at the top. Pour in the water, and stew gently for two and a half hours, keeping the lid of the stewing-pan closely shut. Occasionally shake the pot to prevent burning.

IRISH STEW — ANOTHER WAY
(OUR CAPE RECIPE)

Take ribs of mutton, three or four pounds, brown slightly with a little onion, then add a good soup-plate of potatoes sliced, with a piece of red chilli. Cover the meat with the potatoes and simmer for two hours. Leave the meat whole, only joint it.

J

N.B.—All jams and preserves when made should be put in glass bottles or china pots (previously well scalded). A round of silver paper, large enough to rest on the top of the jam and cover it, should be dipped in brandy and laid on the jam, and the mouth of the jar neatly covered with paper carefully pasted down to exclude the air, and the name and date of the preserve written upon it.

JAM.—*See* Grape Jam and Loquat Jam.

JAM —CAPE GOOSEBERRY (D)

Shell the gooseberries, and give each one a prick with a steel pin. Wash if dusty, then put the fruit in an enamelled or copper saucepan rubbed with olive oil, add just enough water to moisten the gooseberries, and set to boil briskly for 7 or 10 minutes, then add sugar equal to the weight of the raw fruit; let it boil another 10 or 15 minutes. Test if it is good by dishing a little in a saucer and letting it cool; if the syrup has a crinkly or creamy surface it is right, and the syrup must be oily and thick. This is one of our best jams and will keep well.

JAM — LEMON
(AN IMITATION OF SCOTCH MARMALADE)

Ingredients:

8 lb. of carrots
8 lb. of sugar

4 lb. lemons or oranges, or Seville oranges

First boil the oranges and carrots together till nearly soft, in enough water to cover them well. Pour off all the water and keep on one side. Then mince all through the mincing-machine (seeds of the oranges as well). Add the sugar, and four or five cups of the water in which the oranges and carrots were boiled; boil it all clear. Keep the lid on the pot at first, as it is apt to become dry. Before putting in the jam, take care to oil the preserving-pot with olive oil to prevent its burning. (*See also* Marmalade.)

JAM — MARROW, GINGER AND LEMON (D)
(MISS HIGHAM'S)

Ingredients:

Marrow, sugar, lemons. ginger and saffron

Pare the vegetable-marrow, scoop out all the soft seedy part and cut the marrow into pieces about 1 inch thick. Lay these in a pan of cold water with a teaspoon of salt, and let it remain two days, *changing the water daily.* Wipe the pieces dry and weigh.

To every pound of marrow, add 1¼ lb. sugar, 1 oz. whole ginger (cracked), and the juice of a lemon and the peel cut very thinly. Put all the ingredients (*except half of the sugar*) into a preserving pan with a teacupful of water, and 1 dram of saffron tied in a muslin bag (this is taken away when the preserve is sufficiently yellow); boil 1¼ hours, pour into a bowl and cover, and let it remain till the next day. Then boil again, *adding the remainder of the sugar,* for 1½ hours.

The saffron is best steeped in a jar with a little water, and a tiny pinch of citric acid before using—it draws out the colour, and uses less saffron, half a dram being sufficient for 4 lb. vegetable marrow.

JAM — MELON

Ingredients:

6 lb. of ripe melon, minced or cut in slices
4 lb. sugar

A small piece of bruised ginger in a bag

After mincing the melon put it into a preserving-pot (previously oiled). Let it just boil up, then add the sugar. Boil till clear, and the juice nice and thick. Stir repeatedly, or it will burn. Cork well.

JAM — KAFFIR WATERMELON

Take twelve pounds of watermelon, six pounds of sugar, mash through a mincing-machine; also three oranges. Boil up well, then add the sugar. Boil till clear. *A very good jam.*

JAM — ORANGE (D)
(Mrs. Burrel's)

Ingredients:

12 oranges	3 lemons
9 pints water	10 lb. sugar

Cut the oranges and lemons in thin strips, being careful to take out all the seeds. Pour water on the cut up fruit, and let it stand 24 hours. The next day boil for 1½ hours, then add the sugar and boil till the syrup is jellied.

JAM — PEACH
(Cape)

Peel and slice the Clingstone or yellow peach. Have ready a basin of water with a handful of salt in it, lay the sliced peaches for half an hour in this. Take one pound less sugar than fruit, oil the preserving-pot, put alternate layers of fruit and sugar and a few cups of water into the pan. Stew gently till clear, and the syrup thick. *A delicious jam for breakfast or tea.*

JAM — PINEAPPLE

The weight of the fruit in sugar. Make a syrup of the sugar (a cup of water to a cup of sugar).

Peel and slice the pineapples, and preserve in the syrup. The juice of a lemon may be added after it is finished. Takes about three hours.

JAM — QUINCE
(Mrs. Cloete's)

Slice the quinces or pass through a mincing-machine, take the same weight of sugar as fruit. First oil your preserving-pot (very clean copper or enamelled), then put in the cut up fruit. Add a few cups of water, let it boil for half an hour; then add the sugar, and boil till quite clear.

JELLY
(Mrs. Daniel Cloete's)

Ingredients:

2 oz. gelatine	2 lemons
1 lb. brown sugar	The white and shells of 4 eggs
1 pint sherry	A few cloves
½ pint brandy	2 small pieces of mace
The juice of 3 oranges	6 cardamom seeds

Soak the gelatine in one pint of cold water, then pour on half a pint of boiling water to dissolve the soaked gelatine (in winter take one pint or the jelly will be too firm). Then add the other ingredients, and the whites of the eggs well whisked to a stiff froth. Boil on a brisk fire until the scum rises to the top of the saucepan. Have ready a tumbler of cold water, pour some of this water on the boiling jelly. Do this three times, letting it boil in between. Remove from the fire, let it stand five minutes, strain through a jelly bag into a mould, and turn out when cold. *Very good.*

JELLY
(Mrs. Alexander van der Byl's)

Ingredients:

2 quart packets gelatine	15 cloves
6 eggs	2 sticks of cassia (or cinnamon)
1 tumbler lemon juice	The peel of a lemon
1 bottle sherry	The shells of 3 eggs, broken quite
2 wineglasses French brandy	fine
12 tbsps. of brown sugar	

Put one cup of cold water on two quarts of gelatine to soak; when well soaked, pour in three cups of boiling water. Whisk the whites of the eggs to a froth; then add wine, brandy, the lemon or orange peel, and all the other ingredients. Stir all the ingredients well. Let it boil up three times, take it from the fire, pour on it one cup of cold water, and let it stand for five minutes; then strain through jelly-bags till quite clear, and pour into moulds. *Good.*

Half a tumbler of lemon and half orange-juice may be used instead of one whole tumbler of lemon-juice.

JELLY — ASPIC
(Mrs. Cloete's)

Two and a half ounces gelatine soaked in a cup of cold water; one quart boiling water; ten peppercorns; ten allspice; two cloves; one onion; one dessertspoonful salt; two bay leaves; a small cup of Tarragon vinegar; juice of one lemon; whites of two eggs well whisked; one tumbler of cold water poured in while boiling, to clarify. Strain through jellybag till clear. *Enough for fourteen persons.*

75

JELLY — ANOTHER ASPIC OR SAVOURY

Ingredients:

1 calf's foot	1 blade of mace
6 oz. ham	10 peppercorns
2 lb. of veal	Whites of 2 eggs
1 large carrot	1 tsp. of Tarragon vinegar
1 small onion	1 sp. isinglgass
1 bunch of sweet herbs	Half a gallon of water

Put about six ounces of ham, two pounds of knuckle of veal, and a calf's foot (with the bone broken) into a stew-pan, with one large carrot, a small onion, and a bunch of sweet herbs, and the water. Boil it until reduced to one quart; strain it through a sieve. When cold, skim off all the fat, and put the jelly into a stewpan with the whites of two eggs (well whisked), a teaspoonful of Tarragon vinegar, and a spoonful of isinglass. Stir it until on the point of boiling, then draw it to the side, and let it *simmer gently* for nearly twenty minutes. Let it stand to settle, and then pour through a jellybag until quite clear, when it will be fit to use for garnishing meat pies, etc. Time, one and a half hours.

JELLY — BLACKBERRY, IN A MOULD
(MRS. JACKSON'S)

Ingredients:

2 lb. of blackberries	½ oz. gelatine
¼ lb. of white sugar	

Extract the juice from the fruit by putting in the oven in a jar for a few hours; strain through a muslin bag placed over a colander or strainer. Soak half an ounce of gelatine in a little water; add to the blackberry juice, with a quarter of a pound of sugar; boil all for half an hour. Put in a wet mould; turn out next day; serve with cream. This will do for mulberries, only taking more sugar.

JELLY — ANOTHER BLACKBERRY (D)
(MISS ADEANE'S)

Take the fruit before quite ripe, put it in a pot and tie up close and place it in a kettle of water. Leave the fruit so till it is reduced to pulp, then strain, and to a pint of juice add 1 pound of powdered sugar. Boil till it jellies when cold. Blackberry jelly is an excellent filling for sandwich cakes.

JELLY — CALVES FOOT

Take four calves' feet, slit them in two, take away the fat from between the claws, wash them well in lukewarm water, then put them in a large stew-pan, and cover with water. When the liquor boils, skim it well, and let it boil gently six or seven hours, that it may be be reduced to about two quarts, then strain it through a sieve, and skim all the oily substance which is on the surface of the liquor. If you are not in a hurry, it is better to boil the calves' feet the day before you make the jelly, as, when the liquor is cold, the oily part being at the top, and the other being firm, you may remove every particle of the oily substance without wasting any of the liquor with pieces of kitchen paper applied to it. Put the liquor into a stew-pan to melt, with a pound of lump sugar, the peel of two lemons, and the juice of six, the whites and shells of six eggs (beat together), and a bottle of sherry or madeira. Whisk the whole together until it is on the boil, then put it at the side of the stove, and let it simmer a quarter of an hour. Strain through a jellybag; what is strained *first* must be poured into the bag again, until it is as bright and as clear as spring water. Then put the jelly into moulds to get firm and cold. When it is required to be very stiff, half an ounce of isinglass may be added when the wine is put in. It may be flavoured by the juice of various fruits, etc., or spices, and coloured with saffron, etc.

N.B.—Ten sheep's trotters, which may be bought for twopence-halfpenny will give as much jelly as a calf's foot, which costs a shilling.

FRUIT IN JELLY

Put an inch of jelly into a mould; when set, arrange any fruit you like. Put spoonfuls of jelly in between, to keep in place. It must be done slowly, allowing the jelly to set before adding the fruit. Fill up with jelly. It is an improvement to steep the fruit in maraschino, or brandy, before putting into the jelly.

JELLY — GUAVA
(Mrs. Hiddingh's)

Take nice ripe guavas, peel them, cut them through, and just cover them with water. When quite soft, pour them into a large, coarse bag, something like a jelly-bag, leaving them to drain all night. Next day, convert into jelly by adding to every two cups of the juice, when it boils, one cup of sugar. Boil briskly till the consistency of jelly. Pour a little into a tumbler of cold water; if it *does not* mix with the water, it is ready to be poured into moulds or jars.

JELLY — GUAVA
(Mrs. Hiddingh's) (D)

Take 50 medium-sized guavas, and without peeling them slice them in half-inch rounds; put them in a preserving pot with enough water to cover them well. Boil slowly till the fruit is soft, and then strain through an enamelled colander (as tin discolours guavas), or a piece of coarse white muslin. The next day take 2 cups of sugar to every 3 cups of guava juice and boil briskly. When it bubbles up very quickly and froth sputters up, put a little on a flat plate, and if it gathers a sort of cream and hardens quickly it is good, and should be of a rich dark ruby colour.

JELLY — MEDLAR (D)
(Lady Angela Goff's)

Simmer ripe medlars with sufficient water to cover them slowly till the fruit pulps; strain through a bag, and to a pint of liquor add $\frac{3}{4}$ lb. loaf sugar. Boil for half an hour, skimming the top, but do not stir after it begins to boil. Boil it fast. When cold it will be stiff.

JELLY — MEDLAR
(A Swellendam Recipe)

Let the medlars be quite soft; cut off the tops, put in a preserving-pan, cover with water, boil six or eight hours slowly, strain through a coarse sieve. To every pint of juice add one pound of sugar. Boil over a quick fire, stirring all the time. When it thickens drop on a plate; if it jellies it is done. Or drop into a tumbler of cold water; if it does not mix with the water it is good. *This jelly is delicious, and ought to be a clear amber colour.*

JELLY — QUINCE
(Mrs. Cloete of Constantia's)

Take about twenty-five quinces, wipe them clean, cut in quarters, lay in a large preserving-pot, cover with water (about six quarts to twenty-five quinces); boil till *quite soft*, then strain through a thin cloth, or coarse milk strainer. To three cups of juice take two of white sugar; boil in small quantities on a brisk fire. When it begins to get thick, pour a little into a tumbler of water; and if it congeals, and does not mix with the water, it is ready to be put into moulds or cups. Cover with paper dipped in brandy, and keep in a dry place. *Will keep for years.*

JELLY — SAVOURY MEAT (D)
(MRS. MITCHISON'S)

Ingredients:

½ packet of gelatine
2½ pints of water
1½ lb. shin of beef or gravy
1 carrot
1 onion
A little celery
A blade of mace

20 peppercorns
A few sweet herbs
A tsp. of salt
3 hard-boiled eggs
Any remains of cold chicken or lamb

Cut up the meat overnight into pieces an inch square, put into a saucepan with a quart of water, bring it slowly to the boil, and skim; then add vegetables and salt and simmer for five hours, when the liquid will be reduced to one pint; if it be less, add a little water; strain into a basin. Next day remove the fat; soak half a packet of gelatine, or if the weather is hot a little more, in a pint of cold water. Boil up the stock, then pour into a basin to cool; flavour with a little tomato sauce, lemon or Worcestershire sauce. Pour a little of this jelly into a mould, and when it is set, put some slices of hard-boiled egg on it, fill up with more jelly and more hard-boiled egg, pieces of veal, ham, or sausage, slices of tomato, if in season, or beetroot, adding jelly alternately and finishing up with jelly.

JELLY — SAVOURY MEAT (D)

It is necessary that the stock used for an aspic should be very strong, consequently it will be found better to clear it with raw meat instead of the white of an egg, as the meat always adds more flavour than it takes away in the process of clearing. No turnip should ever be boiled in the stock of which aspic is made, as it is apt to turn it sour. All vegetables have this tendency in some degree, but none to the same extent as the turnip.

JUNKET
(MRS. HIDDINGH'S)

Ingredients:

1 quart of new milk
1 oz. of white sugar

1 tbsp. of Van der Hum
1 tbsp. of rennet

Take new milk, sweeten with one ounce of sugar, let it come to *blood heat;* flavour with a tablespoonful of Van der Hum or rum, one tablespoonful of rennet. Stir well, pour into a glass dish, and stand in a tin of lukewarm water, so that the mixture remains warm for half an hour, in which time it becomes quite firm. Whisk up half a pint of cream with sugar and pour over the junket before serving.

K

KABABS.—*See* Sasaties.

KEDGEREE
(An Indian Way of Dressing Cold Boiled Fish. Mrs. Christian's)

Ingredients:

½ lb. of boiled fish	2 oz. butter
¼ lb. rice	A little cayenne, pepper, salt, and
2 eggs	nutmeg

Wash and boil the rice; break the fish in pieces, taking out all the bones; put the butter, fish, and rice into a stewing pan with cayenne, salt, and a *little* nutmeg. Stir well, then add the eggs well beaten. Stir over the fire until quite hot. Serve in a hot dish. *A nice breakfast dish.*

KEDGEREE — ANOTHER
(For Breakfast. Indian)

Ingredients:

1 tbsp. of rice	A lump of fresh butter
4 hard-boiled eggs	Pepper salt
Any white fish previously boiled	

Boil the rice very soft and dry; boil the eggs hard, and chop them fine; take the remains of any fish that has been previously boiled, mince fine, and mix all well together. Put the mixture in a stewing pan with a lump of fresh butter, stew till thoroughly hot, stirring constantly to prevent burning, season with pepper, salt, and cayenne. Take care not to make it too moist. (Boiled *snoek* or kabeljou, if at the Cape, or any white fish will do.) Time, six minutes after the rice is boiled.

KIDNEYS — BROILED
(For Breakfast)

Take four sheep's kidneys; with a sharp knife cut each kidney lengthways down to the root, but do not separate them; skin them and put a skewer under the white part of each to keep them flat. Make the gridiron warm and rub it over with butter; place the kidneys with the inside downwards, and broil them over a clear fire. When sufficiently done on one side, turn on the other. Remove the skewer, season with pepper and salt, put a little piece of butter in the centre of each, and serve on a piece of well-buttered toast. They must be sent to the table as hot as possible.

KIDNEYS — STEWED
(Mrs. Fleming's)

Parboil some sheep's kidneys, divide them, toss in a pan with some pepper, salt, cayenne and flour, and a piece of butter. Then take a few spoonfuls of stock, a little sherry, minced parsley, and half a teaspoonful of Worcestershire sauce. Simmer gently (*but do not boil*) for fifteen minutes.

KIDNEYS AND EGGS (D)
(A Breakfast Dish. Mrs. Becker's)

Lay four kidneys for a few minutes in warm water, draw off the skins, cut the kidneys in half, and roll them in fine bread-crumbs, seasoned with cayenne or ordinary pepper and salt. Fry them slowly in butter or dripping till nice and tender; cut in tiny dice. Take four eggs, beat them up with a little milk, then mix in the minced kidneys and fry all in a pan as you would " scrambled eggs," and pour over squares of toast, buttered, before serving. This quantity makes a large dish.

KOESISTERS
(Batavian or Old Dutch Sweetmeat Recipe)

Ingredients:

3 breakfast-cups of flour	1 tsp. of mixed spices
1 cup brown sugar	4 eggs well beaten
2 tsps. of cinnamon	Half a cup of fat and butter melted
1 tbsp. of yeast	

Knead all well together, and let it stand for half an hour, then roll out on a board made for the purpose. Cut each about an inch and a half long, let them boil in fat. When done, dip the cakes into a syrup made of three cups of sugar and two of water, well boiled and flavoured with cinnamon. *Will keep for months.*

KONFYT — LIME OR LEMMETJIES (D)

Pare the limes very thinly and lay them in fresh cold water for 3 days. Then remove from water and cut a cross at one end of each lime, put them in a preserving pan with cold water, and set them to boil until they can be easily pierced with a thin straw. Take them out of the pan, and put immediately into cold water. After a few minutes take them out and drain well. In the meanwhile make a clear syrup by taking dry white sugar (of the same weight as the fruit), and water in equal proportions, set it to boil, and when clear, strain through muslin; allow it to get cold, then put in the pan again with the fruit boiling gently, until quite tender and transparent. Should the fruit be quite done before the syrup is thick enough, remove and boil the syrup alone until of the proper consistency, after which the fruit can be added again and allowed to simmer for a little while. Boiling it too fast or too long will harden the fruit and give it a brown colour, instead of green.

KONFYT.—*See* Preserves.

81

KREEF — POTTED
(Cape Crawfish)

Boil the kreef, mince in the sausage machine, adding all the red meat. For one pound of minced kreef, two blades of mace, one teaspoon black pepper, half a teaspoonful of salt, some cayenne, three ounces butter, one ounce sheep-tail fat. Mix the spices with the crawfish; work all well together. Bake the whole in a pie-dish in a moderate oven until nearly brown. *To be eaten cold.*

L

LAMB — STEWED WITH PEAS

Ingredients:

The scrag or breast of lamb	A little butter and flour
1 quart of green peas	A small onion
Salt, pepper	

Joint the breast of lamb, lay it in a stewing pan with enough water to cover it. Slice the onion and put it over the meat. Cover the saucepan close, and let it stew or simmer for twenty minutes; take off the scum. Add salt, and the quart of green peas (shelled). Cover the pot, and let it stew for half an hour. Work a spoonful of flour into a lump of butter, and stir it into the stew; add pepper, and let it stew for ten minutes longer. Time, one hour.

LEMON CHEESE (D)

Take 2 lemons and rub off the rind with sugar—as much sugar as would absorb the oil in the rind. Put the sugar in a basin, add to it a pint of good cream, the juice of two large lemons, and 2 tablespoonfuls of brandy. Whisk it well for 10 minutes. Lay a piece of gauze in the inside of a sieve, then pour the mixture into the gauze to drain. It must be made the day before being used.

LEMON.—*See* Cream.

LEMON CREAM WITHOUT CREAM (D)

Ingredients:

½ lb. sugar	The whites of 3 eggs and the yolk of one
½ pt. boiling water	The juice of 3 lemons

Dissolve the sugar in the boiling water, and when cool add the egg beaten, then the lemon-juice. Strain the mixture into a jug and set it in a pan of boiling water, stirring it continuously one way till it is of the thickness of custard. Will keep some days in cool weather.

LETTUCE — BRAISED (D)

Wash the lettuces well and boil them two minutes, then place in a pan of cold water. Drain off all the water and place them in a Yorkshire-pudding tin, with bacon top and bottom, onions and carrots and a bay leaf. Cover with paper and bake one hour. Dish up with good gravy. (Useful when there are many lettuces in the garden which threaten to run to seed before they can be used.)

LIME WATER

Two tablespoonfuls of fine lime to a quart of boiling water. Mix well, and when the lime has drained to the bottom pour the clear water into a bottle; cork and keep for use. A tablespoonful taken in milk is very good for indigestion. (Prepare lime water for Mebos this way.)

LIQUEUR — ORANGE
(MRS. MYBURGH, ELSENBURG, OLD DUTCH)

Ingredients:

5 bottles of brandy	4 lb. of white loaf sugar
9 sweet oranges (peel and juice)	A few sticks of cinnamon

Cut four incisions in the oranges and squeeze them slightly, then let all soak together for ten days, then bottle.

LIQUEUR — ANOTHER ORANGE
(OLD COUNTRY)

Peel very thinly ten oranges and ten lemons. Put the peel on four bottles of good Cape brandy, add four pounds of white sugar. Let it stand for eight or ten days, stirring every day, morning and evening. Strain and bottle.

LIQUEUR — VAN DER HUM
(MRS. CLOETE. ANOTHER OLD RECIPE)

Dissolve three pounds of candied sugar in six bottles of good brandy (*best Cango will do*). Then mix with it one hundred cloves, a quarter of a pound of cinnamon, twelve tablespoonfuls of finely-cut nartjie-peel, one netmeg, a few cardamom seeds. Let it all stand for a month and a half, shaking occasionally, then bottle. Clarify through filtering papers. The brandy should not be weaker than 22 degrees, or the liqueur will not be clear. *Also good.*

LIQUEUR — VAN DER HUM
(OLD RECIPE. CAPE SPÉCIALITÉ)

Ingredients:

10 bottles of brandy	50 cloves
10 dessertsps. of cinnamon, just bruised	20 tbsps. finely-cut nartjie peel
	Half a nutmeg

Mix all well together, and allow the ingredients to remain on the brandy for one month till all the virtue is extracted. Then take five pounds of *clear* light brown crystallized sugar, boil to a *thick* rich syrup. When quite cold, mix one cup of syrup to two of the spiced brandy, stir well till quite mixed. Add one wineglass of best rum to *every* bottle of Van der Hum. The rum mellows the mixture. Put all back into a cask, and clarify with the whites of two eggs well whisked, and lightly put on the top of the cask. In three weeks it will be beautifully clear and ready for bottling. If made in small quantities, the brandy and spices can be put in jars well corked, and the spices in little bags. *Very good.*

LOAF — TO FRESHEN A STALE

Dip quickly into cold water and put into a moderately warm oven for twenty minutes. This quite freshens any stale loaf.

LOQUAT JAM
(Frances Cloete's)

Ingredients:

6 lb. of fruit	8 lb. of white crystallized sugar

Peel and stone the loquats; put them into the preserving-pan in layers. Boil quickly for three hours. If the fruit is nice and ripe take equal quantities of sugar.

LUNCHEON DISHES.—*See also* Chestnut Chipolata, Bredies, Calf's Head. Curries, Cutlets, Irish Stew, Lamb (Stewed), Fish Dishes, Eggs (Curried), Smoorvis, Soused Fish, Hearts (Sheep), Heatherton, *see under* Entrées.

M

MACARONI CHEESE (D)
(Miss le Sueur's)

Ingredients:

2 oz. macaroni	1 pint milk
3 oz. grated cheese	Mustard, cayenne pepper
½ oz. butter	3 more oz. grated cheese

Pour boiling water on the macaroni, let it stand for half an hour. Set the milk to boil, and stir into it gently the soaked, strained macaroni, letting it boil till the macaroni is soft and all the milk is absorbed. Then stir in the cheese, mustard, pepper, and butter. Put into a pie-dish, sprinkle the second lot of cheese over all, and bake a light brown. Serve *very hot.*

MACAROONS
(Mrs. Myburgh's, a very old Dutch Recipe)

Take one pound of almonds, blanched and pounded, and one pound of sugar. Melt the sugar and almonds over the fire till quite a *tough* jelly. Then have ready the whites of four eggs beaten to a froth, whip together when cold. This way of melting the sugar and almonds is excellent, as it prevents the macaroons from running together in the tins. Dust some fine cinnamon over. The old-fashioned way was to put a small piece of citron preserve on every cake. When pounding the almonds add a spoonful of rose-water.

MACAROONS — ANOTHER RECIPE
(Mrs. J. Cloete's)

Ingredients:

1 lb. almonds blanched and pounded	The whites of 2 eggs
1 lb. sifted sugar	¼ tsp. of cinnamon

Blanch and pound the almonds, adding a little rose-water while pounding. Mix with the sugar, which should be slightly warmed, then stir the white of the eggs well whisked. Butter a paper and lay it on a baking-pan; with a fork put small lumps of the paste on the paper. Bake in a moderately slow oven for twenty minutes. A small piece of candied citron stuck into each little cake is a great improvement. *Very good.*

MARINADE — FOR FISH, GERMAN (D)
(Mrs. Carl Becker's)

Ingredients:

½ pint of vinegar	1 quart water
A few bay leaves	¼ oz. salt
A small white onion, sliced	½ oz. butter
1 doz. peppercorns	1 doz. allspice
3 cloves	

Boil all these together about a quarter of an hour, to get out the flavour. Then put into this mixture half a Stockfish, or Kabeljou, and after boiling up another quarter of an hour, leave it to get cold in the spiced water mixture, and serve with mayonnaise sauce.

MARMALADE OR CHEESE — APRICOT
(Cape. Mrs. Henry Cloete's)

Two hundred apricots, wiped and cut into pieces, their weight in sugar. Slightly wipe the preserving-pan with Lucca oil. Put in the apricots, let them boil to a pulp, stirring all the time. Then add the sugar; stir well. Let the whole boil briskly till a clear golden brown.

It is ready to dish when in passing a spoon through the mixture it opens dry from the pot as it were. Put into moulds or basins; keeps beautifully. Some of the pips blanched, and cut up in the marmalade, is liked by some people. Six pounds is a nice quantity to boil at a time. Use an enamelled or copper preserving-pan; it will take about two hours altogether to preserve.

MARMALADE — ORANGE
(MRS. SHAW'S)

Ingredients:

12 large oranges	8 lb. sugar
12 pints of water	

Cut the oranges in thin slices, and then soak in water twenty-four hours. Then add the sugar, and boil till it becomes a jelly.

Lemons may be done the same way.

MARMALADE (D)
(MRS. MARSHALL'S)

Ingredients:

12 Seville oranges	3 lemons

Divide the oranges into quarters and slice them all through into thin slices. Put the pips into a basin. To each pound of fruit add $2\frac{1}{2}$ pints of water. Let it stand 24 hours. Then boil the mixture slowly till the fruit is perfectly soft. Let it stand again 24 hours.

Meanwhile the pips in the basin have been covered with water for 48 hours. Strain out the pips and add this water to the marmalade mixture, which weigh and add an equal weight of sugar. Boil $1\frac{3}{4}$ hours, or until it jellies.

MARMALADE — SCOTCH
(MRS. ETHERIDGE'S)

Ingredients:

6 lb. of Seville or bitter orange	12 lb. of sugar

Scrape or grate the peel slightly; put the oranges into a stewpan; *cover* them with cold water. Boil gently for two hours, keeping them well under water with a plate on the top. When quite soft take them out and drain. Open them, and take out the seeds. Cut the peel and pulp all together in thin strips (some people mince everything through a mincing-machine). For every pound of fruit, weighed *after being boiled*, take two of sugar, and one pint of the water the oranges were boiled in. Boil all together for half an hour, and pour the marmalade boiling hot into jars.

MARMALADE.—*See also* Jams and Preserves.

MAYONNAISE — FOR COLD CHICKEN
(Mrs. Fleming's)

Ingredients:

2 eggs
Some Lucca oil
2 tbsps. of vinegar
1 tsp. of salt

1 tsp. of sugar, mustard, cayenne
Some cold chicken
2 tbsps. of cream

First prepare the following mayonnaise mixture: Beat the yolks of two eggs well; add gradually drop by drop Lucca oil, until it is worked into a stiff ball, then gradually add the vinegar, salt, mustard, and cayenne, until the sauce is thin enough to *pour* over the meat, in the consistency of cream. At the last moment before pouring over the meat, add two tablespoonfuls of cream. Sufficient for one mayonnaise.

Remove all the meat from the bones, put into a pie-dish. Pour over it about a dessertspoonful of oil, a tablespoonful of vinegar, a teaspoonful of chopped onions, and some parsley, pepper and salt. Leave this for half an hour. Remove the meat *from this* when you want to arrange the mayonnaise. Put alternate layers of meat, lettuce, beetroot, on a dish, pouring the mayonnaise mixture over each layer. Garnish with hard-boiled eggs, olives, anchovies. A few capers are an improvement.

MAYONNAISE. — *See* Sauces for *Other Recipes.*

MEAT LOAF — BLIND HARE (D)
(Mrs. Becker's)

Ingredients:

1½ lb. steak finely minced, or mutton
2 slices stale bread, soaked in milk,
    and squeezed dry
8 cloves, finely pounded, and a few
    coriander seeds
¼ egg-spoon of ground pepper

Salt
A dash of nutmeg
½ oz. butter or dripping
Thin slice onion, minced
Yolk of an egg

Mix all these ingredients well together, and shape the mixture into a little roll, put in an enamelled pie-dish, cover with a lattice of strips of bacon, and bake for an hour and a quarter in a good hot oven. To the gravy in the dish (the roll having been put on a hot meat-dish and kept hot) add a little stock, and, if you have it, some cream, and just let the gravy boil up. This meat loaf is very nice cold, and is excellent for picnics.

MEBOS.—*See* Apricots, Dried and Salted.

MERINGUE
(Mrs. D. Cloete's)

Ingredients:

¼ lb. of sifted sugar   The whites of 4 eggs

Whisk the whites of the eggs to a stiff froth, and with a wooden spoon stir quickly the sugar in the whites. Have ready some thin wooden boards, cut strips of paper two inches wide. Place the paper on the board, and drop a tablespoonful of the mixture on the paper, taking care to let all the meringues be of the same size. In dropping it off the spoon give them the shape of an egg. (If a tablespoon is taken and carefully turned over, it is egg-shaped). Keep them two inches apart. Strew over them sifted sugar, and bake in a moderate oven for half an hour. As they begin to colour, take them out of the oven. Take each slip of paper by the two ends, and turn it gently on the table, and with a small spoon take out the soft part of the meringue. Spread some clean papers on the board, turn the meringues upside down, and put them into the oven again to harden and brown on the other side. If kept in a dry place they will keep for weeks. When required for table, fill them with whipped cream flavoured with liqueur (Van der Hum) and vanilla. Join two of the meringues together, and pile them high on the dish. Great quickness is required in making meringues, for if they are not put into the oven *as soon as they are mixed, the sugar melts.* The sweeter the meringues are made the crisper they will be; they are sometimes coloured with cochineal. *This quantity will make two dozen.*

MINCEMEAT

Ingredients:

1 lb. beef suet	¼ lb. candied peel
1 lb. stoned raisins cut in half	1 tsp. of salt
1 lb. currants	2 oz. Scotch marmalade
2 apples, chopped small	1 tsp. powdered cloves
2 lb. castor sugar	½ pint of brandy

Mix all well together. To be made a month before it is used. It will keep for a year if well corked.

MINCEMEAT — ANOTHER
(Mrs. Andrew's)

Ingredients:

3 large lemons	2 lb. moist sugar
3 large apples	1 oz. sliced candied orange-peel
1 lb. stoned raisins	1 teacupful of brandy
½ lb. currants	2 tbsps. orange marmalade
1 lb. chopped suet	

Grate the rind of the lemons, squeeze out the juice, strain it. Boil the remainder of the lemons until tender enough to pulp, also the apples, which are to be mashed. Add the other ingredients one by one; mix all well together, put into jars with closely covered lid. *Excellent.*

MINCEMEAT (D)

Ingredients:

¾ lb. suet

1 lb. currants

½ lb. mixed candied peel

1 nutmeg, grated

The peel and juice of a lemon

1 lb. apples

1 lb. sugar

½ tsp. mixed spice

A tsp. salt

Chop the suet fine; wash and pick the currants, stone the raisins and mince them, peel and core the apples and chop or mince them, cut up the candied peel, grate the nutmeg and the peel of the lemon, then add sugar and spice and mix the whole well together. Put the mixture into jars, pressing it down as closely as possible to exclude the air, and cover with brandied paper.

MINCE PIES

Make some puff paste (which see), roll it out very thinly, less than a quarter of an inch, line your patty-tins (first butter them); fill liberally with mincemeat. Cover with a thicker layer of puff paste, brush over with an egg well whisked. Bake in a brisk oven for twenty-five minutes. Sprinkle or sift very fine sugar over them. The pies may be warmed up if made a day or two before wanted.

The pies may be made *like open tarts*, and burnt brandy handed with them.

MOSBOLLETJIES
(OLD DUTCH, MRS. MOORREES'S)

Ingredients:

2 lb. of raisins

16 lb. flour

3¼ lb. sugar

8 eggs

1½ lb. butter

1 lb. fat

2 tbsps. aniseed

2 nutmegs, grated

1 tbsp. ground cinnamon

Mosbolletjies — so-called from "Mos," juice of the grape in its first stages of fermentation, and " Bolletjie," a bun. During the wine-making season the freshly fermented grape-juice is commonly used instead of yeast by the country people of Stellenbosch, Fransch Hoek, etc., and very nice buns, etc., are made with it. When grapes are not to be had, we take raisins, as in the following recipe, and put them in a jar which is previously seasoned by having had fermented raisins or grapes in it. This jar is not *washed* with water, but generally dried in the sun and kept closely covered from dust, and only used for making the " mos " in, as one is so much surer of its fermenting in a given time if made in a seasoned jar or calabash.

Cut raisins or mince them, put them in a jar or calabash, with twelve cups of lukewarm water, on the stove or *warmest* part of your kitchen for twenty-four hours, till they ferment. Have ready the flour, in which, after being well mixed with the sugar, spices, etc., make a hole; into this strain the fermented juice of the raisins. Sprinkle some flour over the top, and set to rise for some hours in a warm place. Then melt the butter and fat, warm the milk, whisk the eight eggs, yolks and whites separately. Mix the whole well together into a stiff dough, knead with the hand for quite three-quarters of an hour, let it stand overnight to rise. In the morning, roll the buns, set in buttered pans in a warm place, let them rise for half an hour. Brush with the yolk of an egg, and some milk and sugar. Bake for half an hour in an oven heated as for bread. To dry, cut into two or three when cold, and put into a cool oven overnight. *Very good.*

MUSHROOMS — FRIED

Take large " flap " mushrooms, peel carefully; fry in a pan, with pepper and salt, in boiling lard or butter, and serve on toast very hot. (As a vegetable or as a breakfast dish.)

MUSHROOMS — STEWED
(My Mother's)

Ingredients:

Button mushrooms	Some fine bread-crumbs
Salt to taste	A tbsp. of cream
1 oz. of butter	Pepper, a little nutmeg

Wash and thoroughly cleanse the mushrooms of sand; put them in a stewing pan with the lid closed, let them simmer till tender. Then add the butter, rolled in flour, or bread-crumbs, pepper, and nutmeg. Boil for ten minutes. When ready to dish, stir in the cream or the yolk of an egg. (To eat with meat, or as a breakfast dish.)

MUSHROOMS — STEWED

Clean and wipe your mushrooms well. For every three large mushrooms or six buttons take a dessertspoonful of cream, a seasoning of cayenne and salt, or nutmeg and pepper if preferred. Stew for half an hour, till nice and tender. Serve on hot devilled toast with crust cut off. *Good.*

MUTTON.—*See* Saddle.

MUTTON CHOPS
(A favourite Cape dish)

Cut some nice chops, either from a loin or neck of mutton that has been well hung; beat them well with a wooden kitchen mallet; then dip in boiling fat or lard, then in bread-crumbs (made by drying stale bread in an oven, and pounding it, and keeping ready for use), or fine biscuit, some pepper and salt. Have ready your gridiron, well heated on wood coals; lay your chops on this, and broil a nice brown over a quick fire, turning occasionally. Serve with a mould of mashed potatoes or tomato sauce. *Very good.*

Pork chops done in the same way are very good.

MUTTON CHOPS IN BATTER
(Colonial)

Cut from the tender leg of mutton (uncooked), or loin, nice little slices. Season with pepper, salt, and a little nutmeg. Dip in a batter made of half a pint of milk, three tablespoonfuls of flour, and two eggs (if eggs are scarce, flour mixed with thick milk and half a teaspoonful of carbonate of soda makes a very light, nice batter). Fry in hot dripping or lard, as you would a cutlet.

MUTTON CHOPS IN BATTER — ANOTHER WAY
(For Cold mutton)

From a cold leg of mutton cut slices an eighth of an inch thick. Beat up an egg, stir in a teaspoonful of Worcestershire sauce; dip each slice in this, roll in bread-crumbs. Fry quickly. Serve with fried or mashed potatoes.

MUTTON — CORNED (D)
(Groote Post)

Ingredients:

6 lb. breast of mutton	2 oz. salt
1 oz. brown sugar	½ oz. saltpetre

Cut off all the shoulder-part and joint the mutton before corning. Lay the meat in a flat bowl, first rough-salting it with just a sprinkling of salt and throwing away the liquid formed. Now take a mixture of salt, sugar and saltpetre and rub all well into the meat and leave in the bowl for three days. Then simmer till quite tender when the bones will come out easily. Let it cool, putting a flat plate and a weight on it to flatten it. When cold it can be put on the side-table like a ham, or for breakfast or luncheon, slices are nice grilled, with a sprinkling of bread-crumbs and pepper. When out in the veld picnicking or travelling, slices of corned mutton stuck into a stick cut like toasting-fork and held over a clear-burning fire are very appetizing. As it grills the meat so quickly, chops done like this are are also very nice.

MUTTON — NEAPOLITAN LEG OF (D)
(MY OWN)

Ingredients:

6¼ lb. leg of mutton
Bread-crumbs, suet, sweet herbs, for stuffing flavoured with nutmeg, pepper, salt and a suspicion of onion
2 large onions

Few blades of mace
Some allspice
Macaroni
1 lemon, or a glass of light wine
Yolk of an egg

Bone the leg of mutton, and stuff it with a well-mixed stuffing made of the bread-crumbs, suet, etc. Sew up, and stew the leg with a quart of water with the onions put in whole with just a slit at one end, and the mace and some allspice. About an hour before dinner soak some macaroni by pouring boiling water on it, and add to the liquid in the pot. Add the juice of the lemon, or the wine, and just before serving, the yolk of egg beaten up well to the gravy, and remove immediately without again boiling up. Serve the mutton on a very hot dish, with the onions and macaroni arranged around. This dish takes 2¼ hours to cook.

MUTTON — STEWED CHOPS (D)

Beat the chops with the blunt edge of a knife, then lay them in a little milk for a few minutes. Next lay them in a flat stewing-pot, not a deep saucepan, sprinkle over them a few thin slices of onions fried a nice light-brown, some salt, pepper, a dash of nutmeg, a layer of fine bread-crumbs; repeat layers, same order. Cover close and let it stew gently for half an hour, shake the saucepan, add half a cup of stock or water, and let it stew gently for half an hour or more. Serve as an entrée.

N

NARTJIEKONFYT
(MANDARIN ORANGE PRESERVE. FROM MY GRANDMOTHER'S DUTCH RECIPE BOOK)

Take two pounds more sugar than the weight of the oranges. Rasp the nartjie with a piece of glass (which prevents it tasting of steel) or a blunt knife; cut two slits across the bottom of the nartjie, lay in water for two or three days, giving clean water every day. Boil the syrup, and when tepid pour it over the fruit; leave it for a night; preserve the next day very slowly, only letting it simmer. Repeat the process the third day, then bottle and cork well.

NASTURTIUM SEEDS USED AS CAPERS

Gather the seeds before they are too hard, keep them for a day or two with salt sprinkled over them, then put them into empty pickle bottles; pour boiling vinegar over them and leave them to cool. *When cold*, cork closely.

The nasturtium flowers are very nice to eat with bread and cheese and butter; and look very pretty to hand round on a separate plate, with the cheese and butter, after dinner.

O

OBLIETJIES — OR OUBLIÉS
(AN OLD-FASHIONED RECIPE FOR TEA-CAKES BROUGHT TO THE CAPE BY THE FRENCH REFUGEES)

Ingredients:

2 lb. fine flour	4 eggs
1 lb. castor sugar	2 dessertsps. fine sifted cinnamon
¾ lb. butter	½ pint wine

Beat butter to a cream, mix with the sugar, add eggs, whisked separately, the wine, and lastly the flour, in which the cinnamon has been mixed. If the batter is not quite thin enough to spread, add a little more wine. Bake in an oublié-pan; put about a dessertspoonful on the pan, shut tight and hold over the fire to brown on both sides; it will take two minutes. Open the pan, roll the oublié as you would a pancake, *while hot*. The oubliés ought to be very crisp and light, and as thin as a wafer. Oublié-pans are called by the ironmongers "wafer-pans," and can be obtained in all the English shops, and at Findlay, Koch, Dixie, etc., Cape Town.

OMELETTE — FOR BREAKFAST

Ingredients:

4 eggs	½ pint of new milk
A slice of stale bread	Pepper and salt

Whisk the eggs well; soak the bread in milk, mash very finely, mix with the whipped egg. Fry in a pan with a little butter or fat. (Makes three good omelettes. Time about three minutes each.

OMELETTE — EGG AND OYSTER

Ingredients:

4 eggs	6 large oysters
2½ oz. flour	Pepper and salt
½ a pint of a milk	

Chop up six large oysters; make a batter of the flour and milk. Mix the whole together, and fry in butter or fat slowly. The oysters may be potted or raw.

93

OMELETTE — GERMAN

Ingredients:

2 eggs	¼ pint boiling milk
1 tsp. flour	1 tbsp. sugar
1 tsp. maizena	20 drops vanilla essence
1 tsp. cream	

Mix the yolks of the eggs with one teaspoonful of fine flour and one spoonful of maizena, then the spoonful of cream, then the quarter of a pint of boiling milk, and lastly the whites well whisked. Butter two ordinary kitchen tin plates, pour in the mixture, and bake in a quick oven till set. Then carefully lay on a silver (hot water) dish, put a layer of apricot jam or any other marmalade on it, and cover with the other omelette. (Three omelettes make a nice dish for four or five people. These may be made savoury omelettes by putting salt, pepper, and parsley instead of jam.)

OMELETTE — HAM OR TONGUE
(ENGLISH)

Ingredients:

3 oz. butter	3 dessertsps. of grated ham or tongue
4 eggs	A little pepper and salt

Grate or mince some ready-dressed ham or tongue very fine. Whisk the yolks and whites of the eggs separately, season with pepper and salt; beat well together, stir into the tongue and ham. Put some butter into your omelette-pan, and when it begins to bubble, whirl up the mixture and pour it into the pan. Stir with a spoon one way until it thickens, then fold the edges of the omelette over in an oval form. Brown nicely, and serve as quickly as possible. Pop the dish into a hot oven for a few minutes if not quite brown enough. Time, five or six minutes.

OMELETTE — A GOOD SWEET
(MRS. SPENCE'S)

Ingredients:

6 eggs	1 tsp. of grated lemon peel
3 oz. sugar	3 oz. butter

Whisk the whites to a stiff froth. Have your omelette pan quite hot, put in three ounces of butter, and when it is melted, mix the whites of the eggs with the yolks, sugar and lemon-peel, and pour into the pan, shaking it round till the under side is slightly browned. Then sift sugar over the upper side. Turn it on a dish, fold it over, and put for five minutes in a brisk oven. Serve it immediately, before it can fall.

OLIVES.—*See* Beef Olives.

ONIONS À LA CRÈME

Ingredients:

6 or 8 nice white Spanish onions	¼ pint of cream
1 tbsp. of fine flour or maizena	2 oz. butter

Boil the onions in two or three waters till nice and soft, and also to take off the strong taste; drain them, and lay them in a warmed vegetable dish. Have ready a sauce made of the flour, cream and butter, as follows: Rub the flour and butter well together, then add a few spoonfuls of boiling water. Stir nice and smooth till quite mixed, then add the cream or milk, and keep stirring till nearly boiling. Pour this sauce over the onions, and serve hot. Time, two hours.

ORANGES — BAKED (D)

You just cut the top of the orange *nearly* off (leaving it like a lid with a hinge), and bake the oranges as you would apples, and send them to the table quite hot; to be eaten egg-fashion, with a spoon and sugar; cream, too, if you wish. They are always popular.

ORANGE PRESERVE.— *See* Nartjiekonfyt.

OYSTERS — SCALLOPED

Ingredients:

3 doz. oysters	Pepper
1 teacupful of grated bread-crumbs	A little lemon-juice
2 oz. of fresh butter	

Butter some tin scallop-shells, or, if you have not any, a small pie-dish. Strew a layer of crumbs, then some thin slices of butter, then enough oysters to fill up pie-dish. Cover with bread-crumbs and slices of butter, add pepper, salt and lemon, and some of the liquor kept from the oysters. Put butter over the whole surface, and bake in a quick oven. Brown in the oven. Serve in dish or shell in which it has been cooked. Time, quarter of an hour.

P

PERLEMOEN, OR CAPE SHELLFISH

Five or six large shellfish. Clean by putting the shell in strong lye (boiling water put on wood ashes; half a teaspoon of washing soda will do as well). The shell separates, and the inside easily comes out, and must then be rubbed on a stone, well washed, and beaten with a wooden mallet. Put in a stewing-pot with a little butter or fat, let it simmer for an hour; then stir in a teacup of fine bread-crumbs, two ounces of butter, some nutmeg and white pepper and *just before serving*, a little salt. Be careful to stir occasionally. No water to be added, as it forms a rich gravy of its own, but requires lots of butter. Ought to be as tender as marrow. *A delicious dish.*

N.B.—The Perlemoen, or Klipkous (Stone-stocking), a species of shellfish found on many parts of the South African coast, adhering to the rocks. The shells are lovely, with a mother-of-pearl lining. The fish is most delicious if properly cooked.

PANCAKES
(MRS. BRINK'S, AN OLD RECIPE)

Ingredients:

6 eggs	A little salt
¼ lb. of flour	2 tbsps. of melted butter
1 tea-cup of warm water	1 quart of milk

Whip up the whites and yolks of the eggs separately; stir in the melted butter and flour gradually, then the milk and water; mix very smoothly. Put an omelette-pan on the fire, with a pat of butter or fat. Put in sufficient batter to run over it as thick as a crown piece; shake the pan when you think one side is done, toss it up so as to turn. Sprinkle with sugar or spread with honey, roll up and put on a dish in the oven until you have enough to send in, or place them on a dish, grating some sugar and cinnamon between each, cut in quarters, and send in very hot.

PANCAKES — AUGUSTA'S FRENCH

Ingredients:

2 oz. butter	2 eggs
2 oz. castor sugar	A little essence of almonds
2 oz. flour	½ pint of fresh milk

Beat the butter to a froth; add the sugar, then one egg well beaten with sugar and butter, then the other, then milk; lastly the flour. This paste must be *quite* smooth. Then butter four tin plates. Bake the pancakes in an oven. When ready, put one pancake over the other with apricot jam, or other preserve, between each. Serve with sifted sugar. Time, about fifteen minutes. *Very good.*

PALATES — BEEF
(MRS. HIDDINGH'S)

Ingredients:

4 palates	A seasoning of nutmeg, pepper or
2 oz. butter	cayenne

Four ox palates make a good dish; soak them, and wash *very* clean; then scald them, and scrape off all the rough skin till perfectly white and clean-looking. Then boil gently, in a good quantity of water, *till tender*. Take them out, and press them between two plates; let them cool; cut them into small squares, or any nice shape. Now take sufficient of the stock in which the palates were boiled to cover them; strain; season with nutmeg, pepper, and salt; thicken with fine bread-crumbs or biscuit; add an ounce of butter and a spoonful of cream. Stew the palates gently in this, and serve as an *entrée*.

PANCAKES WITH CHICKEN
(MISS LIESCHING'S OLD-FASHIONED GERMAN RECIPE)

Take one chicken (or white-legged fowl), one ounce of butter, half a pint of good stock, two onions, some white pepper, a grated nutmeg, a little parsley. Cut up the chicken nicely jointed, let it simmer for an hour. Then have ready four pancakes lightly baked and rolled up and cut in halves, and gently laid in the sauce, not to break them, for a few minutes. Serve nicely in an *entrée* dish, and garnish with the pancakes cut in rings. Should the gravy in which the chicken has stewed require thickening, whisk up an egg with a squeeze of lemon, stir it into the stock quickly after the chicken, etc., has been dished, and pour over the whole. *Very good.*

PARSNIPS — STEWED

Ingredients:

4 large parsnips	A piece of butter mixed with flour
½ pint of cream	Grated nutmeg
	Salt

Boil the parsnips till nearly tender; cut them in thin slices, and put them in a stewing-pan with the cream or milk, butter (rolled in flour), nutmeg and salt. Keep shaking the pan till it is well mixed, thick, and smooth. Put in a hot dish, and serve.

PARSNIPS — STEWED, ANOTHER RECIPE
(CAPE WAY)

Take nice tender parsnips, cut them in rings, put them in a stewing-pot in layers, sprinkling some sugar, flour, and a little butter between each; pour a pint of water over it, and let it simmer for two hours, giving the pot an occasional toss.

PASTRY — CUP PASTE FOR FRUIT OR MEAT PIES (D)

Ingredients:

1 large cup of flour	1 large cup of butter (or ½ butter and
1 large cup of milk	½ ox-marrow or lard)

Mix the butter with the flour dry, now *with a knife* beat up with the milk for a few minutes and spread over the pie-dish filled with fruit or meat, and bake very crisp and nice.

PASTRY — GENEVA, TILLYPRONIE (D)

Ingredients:

¼ lb. pounded sugar	¼ lb. flour
3 oz. fresh butter (whisked to a cream)	Yolks of 3 eggs and *well-beaten* whites of 6.

Having worked your butter to a cream, add the sugar to it, then break in the 3 yolks and beat some time. Now flavour it with a tea-spoonful of orange-flower water, or the rind of a lemon, or pounded vanilla. Add the stiffly-beaten egg-whites. Bake in a baking sheet in a moderate oven. (May be used for sweet apricot sandwiches or cut into little tartlets and filled with jam or preserved fruits.)

PASTE — FOURRÉ POLONAISE (D)

Roll pudding is made of the above pastry. As soon as out of the oven, spread rapidly with apricot jam and roll up before it stiffens. When cut across, you should see three layers of jam.

PASTRY — LIGHT
(For Meat Pies, Patties and Sausage Rolls)

Ingredients:

½ lb. flour	2 oz. lard
¼ lb. butter	A little salt

Rub the lard into the salted flour, mix with cold water rather stiffly. Roll out as thinly as you can, and spread all the butter on as you would bread and butter. Now fold the paste in 3 one way and 3 the other way. so that you have 9 folds altogether with layers of butter between. Always roll *from* you, not from side to side; roll lightly and effectually, giving the paste a push from you so that it gets longer and longer. Now fold again in 3 and roll out straight from you. Again fold in 3 and roll. It is now ready for use. *Always take the finest flour for pastry*, because it is most starchy and makes the lightest pastry. *Keep the butter as cool as you can*, this ensures success.

With small or large meat pies *never forget to leave a hole to let out the air*—it is most poisonous and dangerous not to do so. In making sausage-rolls parboil the sausage, and cut it in half length-ways. Roll in the paste and brush over with egg, and see that the oven is *hot; a cool oven spoils pastry!*

PASTE FOR ROLY-POLY, APPLE, OR BEEFSTEAK PUDDING

Ingredients:

6 oz. flour	1 tsp. baking-powder
2 oz. suet	Water to make a tolerably stiff
½ tsp. salt	paste

For roly-poly roll out the crust very thinly, and spread with quince jam or marmalade. Wet the edges to make them adhere and roll up. Have ready a narrow cloth dipped in hot water, and well dusted with flour; put the roly-poly in the middle, and fold round once, and sew together with a needle and thread, tying up the ends securely with thread also. Put in it boiling water and boil at least three hours.

Instead of jam you could sprinkle on the paste 2 tablespoonfuls currants, 2 of chopped apples, 2 of moist sugar, a little mixed spice, cloves, and some almonds chopped. Proceed as before.

PASTRY — CHEAP
(FRENCH)

Ingredients:

¾ lb. of flour	½ lb. of clarified dripping or lard,
½ tsp. of baking-powder	butter, if you have it, is better
1 egg	

Rub the flour, and half the dripping, and baking-powder together, then mix with the egg and as much water as will make it the right consistency. Roll out twice, and spread over it the remainder of the fat or butter. This makes a good pie crust.

PASTRY CRUST FOR BEEFSTEAK PIE OR GERMAN TART

Ingredients:

4 tbsps. flour	1 egg
1 tbsp. of butter, and lard	A little salt
1 tsp. baking-powder	

Rub the butter and lard into the flour, beat up well with a knife after adding the egg and a few spoonfuls of water.

PASTRY — MY OWN RECIPE, GOOD (D)

½ lb. fine flour, 2 oz. lard, and a little salt, rubbed into the flour, then add half a cup of cold water, into which half a lemon has been squeezed, and beat it up with a large knife. Now put it on the pastry-board and roll out—not too thin—then spread a ¼ lb. of butter on the paste and fold it up, and roll out four or five times *from you*, folding up each time.

PASTRY — SUET
(VERY GOOD FOR HOT TARTS AND PIES)

Ingredients:
½ lb. flour   A little salt
¼ lb. suet

Mix the flour with half the suet, then add about half a pint of cold water. Roll the dough, and spread the remaining suet. Repeat this three times. (Pound suet in a mortar, and spread like butter on puff paste.)

PASTRY — SHORT CRUST (D)

Ingredients:

1 egg	1 lemon
1 oz. sugar	4 oz. butter
6 oz. flour	A little salt

Rub the flour, butter, salt and sugar well together. Break the yolk of the egg in the mixture, add a large spoonful of cold water to the juice of the lemon, and beat all well together with a knife for a few minutes. Roll it out several times and set it to rest for a few minutes before rolling out the pastry very thin and cutting out to line patty pans, etc.

PASTRY — SHORT CRUST, TARTLETS, LEMON CHEESECAKES (D)

Put the yolk of an egg in a basin and stir it round with a wooden spoon for a few minutes, add 1½ oz. castor sugar, and stir till light and creamy, then add the grated rind of a lemon and 1 tablespoon lemon juice. Stir well and mix with half-an-ounce of fine biscuit-crumbs. Then stir in the stiffly whipped white of the egg lightly. After filling the patty-pans with the mixture bake them in a quick oven for fifteen minutes. Serve cold.

PASTRY — SHORT CRUST, SWEETMEAT, AN OLD-FASHIONED) (D)

Use the above short crust for the following old-fashioned sweetmeat. Have ready a mixture of the following:
50 unblanched almonds minced through a mincing-machine.
1 oz. finely shredded citron preserve.
2 oz. sifted sugar.
½ teaspoonful of finely-pounded cinnamon.
Mix all with the well-whisked white of an egg. Roll out the pastry thinly, cut it in lengths of 4 inches by 3. Put a teaspoonful of this mixture in each square of pastry and roll up as you would roly-poly, and twist round to form a ring. Brush with yolk of egg, and bake in a quick oven.

PASTRY.—*See* Pie Crust.

PATTIES
(TANTE KATJE'S)

Ingredients:

Cold meat, minced
1 slice of bread, soaked in milk
Some lemon juice, and some of the
    rind rasped

1 egg
A pinch of pepper and salt
A little nutmeg

Take pie crust, cut into round shapes by putting a small tumbler on it; on each round put a good teaspoonful or more of the above ingredients well mixed together, and cover with another piece of crust, brush with egg, and bake in a hot oven.

PATTIES — LOBSTER
(MRS. FLEMING'S)

Chop up a lobster with red part and spawn; add grated bread-crumbs, salt, pepper, a small lump of butter, chopped sweet herbs. Make the whole into a paste with the yolk of one egg; shape into little flat pieces and fry in lard or butter.

PATTIES — OYSTER

Take potted oyster; mix in the liquid a good lump of butter, some salt, pepper, a tablespoon of cream. Put into little tins lined with puff paste; cover with the same. Bake in a quick oven.

PEARS — STEWED
(MRS. ETHERIDGE'S)

For every pound of pears take half a pound of sugar (soft white) to make a syrup, taking the same quantity of water as sugar. Boil till clear, pour boiling hot over the pears; cover the stewing-pan close. Then boil briskly at first, then moderately, for four or five hours. Add the juice and peel of a lemon; and when nearly done, a glass of dark wine. *Excellent.*

PEARS — STEWED, IN JELLY (D)

Lay each half of a stewed pear in a saucer, with the round side downwards ; the saucer is filled with pink jelly to the brim, and turned out when cold in a pretty shape with the pear right side up. Serve with whipped cream.

PEAS — GREEN, TO BOIL

Shell your peas as *soon* as you have gathered them (*if possible*). For a large vegetable dish of peas take a quart of water, into which put a pinch of salt, and a small piece of vegetable charcoal. Boil for fifteen minutes, if young and fresh, in an *open saucepan*. When tender, drain through a colander, and put in a dish with a piece of butter. If the peas have been gathered some time before being shelled they will have lost their sweetness, in which case add a teaspoonful of sugar. Shake well together in the dish, and keep the dish on the top of the saucepan for five minutes to melt the butter and sugar before serving.

PICKLE — CABBAGE

Take cabbage cut in small pieces, green Mealies (heads of Indian corn) in rings ; tiny carrots, green grapes, small onions, green apples cut in strips. Sprinkle well with salt in an earthern basin for a night. Dry two or three days. Then take onions, cut in rings (about half a pound to every three pounds of the other ingredients), fry in a pan, with olive-oil, to a light brown. Take one cup of bruised ginger (dried ginger, not ground fine, but just crushed in a mortar), a few spoonfuls of turmeric, one cup of sugar; mix with three bottles of vinegar. Let it boil, then add cabbage and all the other ingredients; let the whole boil for an hour. Put into stone jars, and cork. *Will keep for years.*

Unripe peaches, cut in quarters, sprinkled with salt and dried, make a most delicious pickle with the same sauce.

Another similar recipe adds two ounces of coriander seed and two ounces of mustard to the sauce.

PICKLE — RED CABBAGE — ATJAAR (D)
(MALAY)

Cut the cabbage into strips, removing the hard stems, sprinkle salt over it and leave until the next day, then drain and lay open on a cloth to dry. When all the moisture has disappeared, put it into sufficient boiling vinegar and allow to boil for a minute or two, adding a few small pickle onions, some red chillies, and some allspice. When cold, bottle and cork well.

PICKLE — PEACH
(MRS. JACKSON'S)

Ingredients:

2 lb. dried peaches soaked in vinegar for a night	1 tbsp. of mustard seeds
6 large onions, fried a light brown in Lucca oil	6 red chillies (cut up)
	2 oz. curry-powder
1 tbsp. of coriander seeds	$\frac{1}{4}$ lb. brown sugar
6 large pieces of ginger	$\frac{1}{2}$ lb. salt
	1 tbsp. of pepper

Crush all the spices. Boil all the ingredients in three quarts of vinegar till the peaches are nice and soft.

PICKLE — YELLOW PEACH (D)
(FROM AN OLD CAPE FAMILY RECIPE)

Take 50 peaches, peel and slice into four or five pieces each, and sprinkle a little salt on each layer of peaches as you put them in a bowl, where you leave them for a day or two. Then drain the sliced peaches and put them on a clean cloth to dry for a day or two—not more—in the sun. Next take 4 or 5 onions, cut them in slices, and fry light-brown in olive-oil; lastly, take 2 bottles of good vinegar and put into an enamelled saucepan with one dozen red chillies, a few cloves of garlic, a tablespoonful of cracked ginger, a large table-spoonful of turmeric to give it a good colour, and you may add twenty-five *small* onions, if wished. Boil these ingredients, stirring well. Pour the *boiling vinegar*, in which are all the ingredients, on the peaches, and let them boil up, put in a large jar and stir well. The next day bottle for use.

PIE CRUST.—*See* Pastry.

PIE CRUST
(GOOD HOME RECIPE)
Ingredients:

1 lb. finest flour	1½ tsps. of baking-powder
¾ lb. butter	Some milk and water
¼ lb. lard, or sheep-tail fat	

Rub the baking powder into the flour; mix the lard by rubbing into the flour, then mix the flour with milk and water very lightly, to the consistency of dough—*not too stiff*; then roll out thinly, spread butter all over, dust with flour, roll out again. Repeat the process *till all the butter is used.*

PIE CRUST
(MY RECIPE)
Ingredients:

1 lb. flour	1 teacup of cream
½ lb. butter	1½ tsps. of baking-powder
¼ lb. lard	Cold water

Mix the flour, baking-powder, and lard dry, then moisten with cream and water, roll out, and spread with butter twice. This makes most delicious light puff paste. Bake in a quick oven.

PIE CRUST — CHEAP
Ingredients:

2 cups of flour	1 tsp. of baking-powder mixed with
2 tbsps. of lard	1 pint of cold water

Mix all together and roll out.

PIE — A LUXURIOUS QUAIL (D)

Ingredients:

12 quails	Pâté de foie gras, or some other rich,
Bacon	but not strongly flavoured
Rich stock	stuffing
2 lb. steak	½ a bottle of black Worcestershire
Crust	mushrooms
A small tin of truffles	6 hard-boiled eggs

Put a spoonful of the foie gras or the stuffing inside each cleaned bird, wrapping each in a thin slice of bacon. Add the steak cubed, the truffles, the mushrooms, the eggs halved, some Worcestershire sauce, and fill in with the rich stock. Cover with a good crust and bake slowly.

PIE — OLD-FASHIONED DUTCH — OUDERWETSE PASTEI
(Mrs. J. Cloete's)

Ingredients:

1 chicken	Juice of a lemon
2 onions	1 glass of white wine
1 blade of mace	A little sago and vermicelli
Salt	2 hard-boiled eggs
A little pepper	A few slices of ham
2 oz. butter	A few allspices

Take a chicken, joint and cut into pieces, put into a stewing-pan with one white onion, about one pint of broth or water, a wineglass of white wine; put about five allspice, a blade of mace, and twelve peppercorns into a little muslin bag, and add; let the chicken simmer in this for half an hour, then add two spoonfuls of vermicelli, one spoonful of sago, a good lump of butter; stir carefully, as the sago and vermicelli are apt to burn. Just before taking out of the saucepan, whip the yolk of an egg with the juice of a lemon, stir in with the chicken; it thickens the gravy, and gives a nice creamy look. Let this cool, then put into a pie-dish with slices of hard-boiled egg and ham between, and make a few little balls of butter and flour rolled together, and put in the pie-dish. Cover with pie crust nicely rolled and ornamented. Brush with yolk of egg mixed with milk. Bake in a quick oven for one and a half hours.

Note.—If the chicken is very tender, it can be put into the pie-dish uncooked, and will be equally nice, but will take much longer to bake. The old Dutch way is to have the meat parboiled.

PIE — FISH
(A Cape Dish)

Ingredients:

Remains of cold boiled fish	Tomato sauce
2 onions fried in butter or fat	Mashed potatoes
Pepper, salt, mustard	1 egg

Clear the fish from the bones, and break into little pieces; mix well with the onion, seasoning, butter, tomato sauce, half the egg, and a little of the mashed potatoes; pack in a buttered pie-dish, lay the potatoes on the top, brush with the egg. Bake three-quarters of an hour. *Very good.*

PIE — MACARONI

Ingredients:

¼ lb. Macaroni	1 tsp. of mustard
¼ pint of milk	¼ lb. grated cheese
Pepper, salt, mustard	1 egg

Boil a quarter of a pound of macaroni in water till quite soft, then pour off the water; add a cup of milk, a quarter of a pound of grated cheese, butter and mustard, salt, a pinch of cayenne and white pepper. Let it boil for a minute, then bake in a buttered dish, or one lined with puff paste.

PIE — PIGEON

Ingredients:

4 young pigeons	1 glass of wine
Pepper, salt, gravy	2 oz. of butter

Lay a rim of paste round the sides and edges of a pie-dish. After the pigeons are cleaned, halve them; season as you would any other pie; a few slices of ham, some hard-boiled eggs, a cup of good stock or gravy. Cover with puff paste; ornament the top, and stick four of the little feet out of it. Brush over with egg and milk, bake an hour and a half, with buttered paper, if the oven is very hot, over the pie-crust to prevent its burning.

PIE — STEAK

Cut a steak into thin slices, sprinkle with parsley, mushroom, and onion; season with pepper and salt, rubbing in the seasoning well on both sides; roll up each slice of beef, put into a saucepan on a layer of bacon, and put sufficient water to cover the rolls. Simmer gently with the lid on till tender; put into a pie-dish with a layer of hard-boiled eggs, cover with a good crust. Bake in a quick oven for an hour and a half.

PIE — VEAL KIDNEY

Mince a couple of veal kidneys with the fat; season with nicely-chopped herbs, cloves, nutmeg, pepper, and salt; a little chopped celery may be added; four or five hard-boiled eggs, half a cup of fine bread-crumbs, a wineglass of white wine, and a little stock. Mix all well together, cover with crust. Bake for two hours.

PIGGIE, OR SUCKING-PIG
(A FAVOURITE CAPE DISH)

When the piggie has been well cleaned and washed, make a stuffing of bread-crumbs, suet, some dried sage leaves, pepper, salt, lemon-peel. If eggs are plentiful, then moisten with an egg and some water.

Stuff the pig, sew up with strong thread; truss it as a hare is trussed, with its fore-legs skewered back and its hind-legs forward. Lay it on a trivet, in a dripping-pan, with a pint of water in the pan. Rub piggie all over with butter (or sheep-tail fat), and set it in a hot oven. Will take two hours.

I have heard that rubbing the piggie all over with the white of egg, before roasting, makes it nice and crisp.

POFFERTJIES
(AN OLD DUTCH PUDDING)

Ingredients:

½ lb. of butter	6 eggs
¾ lb. of flour	1 lb. of lard
1 pint of milk or water	

Add the butter to boiling milk or water, then stir into it the flour gradually over the fire till it ceases to adhere to the saucepan or spoon; let the mixture *cool on a dish*, then stir in the eggs, yolks and whites whisked separately. Put the lard into a saucepan; when it *boils* well, put lumps of dough about a teaspoonful at a time into the saucepan, keeping the puffs down with a skimmer (as they will rise to the top of the fat), till they are a light brown colour. Serve hot with sugar.

POLONIES (D)

Ingredients:

12 lb. beef	2 lb. fat (beef fat can be used, or the
Coriander seeds.	fat of the tail of Cape sheep,
Pepper, salt, nutmeg	cut into very small dice, and
A little saltpetre	smoked or dried)

Mince the meat, and flavour to taste, put in sausage-bags procured from the butcher (or, if on a farm, use the ox-guts well cleaned). Tie up in quarter-yard lengths, and hang in the smoke for a day. Boil them up the next day for about 10 minutes, and then hang in a dry place. They will keep for months, and are useful for breakfast, sandwiches, and picnics.

PORRIDGE — FOR BREAKFAST

Ingredients:

2 oz. oatmeal	½ pint new milk
1 pint of water	

Put a pint of cold water into a stewpan over the fire; *as it boils*, dredge in the oatmeal with your left hand, and stir with your right. Boil for twenty minutes. When it is made, send it to table in a soup-plate. To be eaten with a little salt or sugar. Hand round with it a jug of hot or cold milk, or cream.

POTATOES — HOW TO BOIL

Put your potatoes into boiling water with a good teaspoon of salt, boil for twenty minutes; when soft, which can be felt easily by pricking with a fork, pour the water off, put the potatoes back (if with their jackets on) into the saucepan, putting the pot on the stove for a few minutes till the skins burst. If the potatoes are peeled leave them in the colander on the steam; toss them, and send them in looking nice and mealy. The Dutch people serve boiled potatoes with a little melted butter.

POTATO CURRY PIE (D)
(MRS. HILL'S)

Cut the meat up small, fry some onions brown, and the meat with them. Put meat and onions in a pie-dish, and half fill the dish with good gravy in which you have smoothly mixed a dessertspoonful of curry-powder. Cover all over, but not too thickly, with mashed potato with which you have mixed a little of the curry gravy, and bake the pie a nice brown.

POTATOES — SAVOURY
(MRS. MANUEL'S)

Bake your potatoes, then cut in half and scoop out the inside, which mix with a little chopped parsley, onion, nutmeg, cheese, pepper, and salt; put back into the skins, egg and bread-crumb the tops, brown them and serve hot.

SWEET POTATOES STEWED AS A VEGETABLE

Peel and slice about four or five pounds of sweet potatoes; take a cup of sugar, a spoonful of flour, a spoonful of butter, and a little salt. Lay the sliced sweet potato in an enamelled saucepan in layers, sprinkled with sugar, butter, and flour, and when you have put in the last layer pour over it a cup of water. Let it all stew gently, giving the pot a stir occasionally.

To those who like sweet things with meat this is very much liked.

Boiling them in water with their jackets on, peeled before serving, and cut in slices, with melted butter, is another good way of cooking sweet potatoes.

PRESERVE.— *See* Marmalade, Jam, Nartjiekonfyt, Apricots Salted (Mebos), Grapes in brandy.

PRESERVING (D)

The secret of successful preserving is putting both the fruit and afterwards the syrup into the jars at boiling heat, and filling the jars to overflowing and screwing up tightly immediately. The syrup is made of equal proportions of sugar and water: say 6 cups of sugar to 6 cups of water. The fruit should weigh as much as the sugar. The syrup is boiled and strained first, and a third set aside in another pot and kept boiling to cover the fruit when it is set in the jars.

PRESERVING APRICOTS AND PLUMS (D)

Halve and stone the apricots, and put them in two-thirds of the boiling syrup and boil for a few minutes. Have your jars ready and heated, having been previously cleaned, and proceed to fill carefully taking the apricots one by one from the boiling saucepan and transferring to the jar. The jars should stand on an enamelled plate on the stove by your saucepan (this is better than a china plate, which the heat might crack, for the syrup often boils in the jar as you are filling up).

In the meantime the remaining third of the syrup, which you kept separate, is boiling in another saucepan, and as soon as you have filled each jar with apricots, leaving enough space above the top apricot for syrup to cover it, you fill up with pure boiling syrup from the reserve saucepan. This is done for plums as well, because the skins of both apricots and plums are very acid, and if you used the syrup you had boiled them in to fill up the jars, it would not keep so well.

PRESERVE — APRICOT, GREEN
(An old Constantia Recipe)

Ingredients:

100 green or unripe apricots   Their weight in sugar

Prick the fruit with a steel pin, lay them in a deep dish, sprinkle some salt over them (about a dessertspoonful), pour boiling water over them, cover with green vine-leaves (this keeps them green), lay a plate on the top. Now proceed to make the syrup, taking a cup of water to a cup of sugar. When it is boiled and clarified, take the apricots out of the salt water, wash them, and pour the boiling syrup over them. Leave for a night like this. The next day preserve them by gently simmering till the fruit is nice and clear.

PRESERVE — APRICOT, RIPE
(Old Dutch)

Apricots can only be preserved by pouring boiling syrup over them for ten days, boiling the syrup every day; the syrup to be made of sugar, the same weight as the fruit. On the tenth day make a fresh thick syrup; put the apricots in a wide-mouthed jar, pour the thick boiling syrup over them, and cork well.

PRESERVE — APRICOTS IN BRANDY
(MISS DE WET'S)

Ingredients:

6 lb. of ripe apricots or peaches   2½ lb. sugar, boiled to a thick syrup

Wipe your fruit very clean, prick with a steel pin, pack the apricots or peaches in a jar. Take one tea-cup of thick syrup and one tea-cup of brandy, mix well, and pour over each layer of fruit as you put them in your jar. When filled, put a paper between the top of the jar and lid; set the jar in a saucepan of water, and let it heat to *near* boiling point, then remove the paper and lid, and when *cold*, cork well.

PRESERVING GREEN BEANS (D)

In a large earthern jar put some salt, then a layer of freshly gathered green beans, then a sprinkling of salt, and so on till the jar is filled, ending with salt, plenty of it, at the top, and cover. Like this they keep well, and when wanted we take them out, wash them well and lay in water for some time to prevent their being too salt.

PRESERVE — CITRON (D)
(MRS. BREDA'S)

Take the weight of the citron before scraping, as an equal weight of sugar will be required. Pare or scrape the citrons with a medium-sized grater, then lay them whole in a deep bowl, and after sprinkling 2 or 3 oz. salt over them, cover the citrons with a plate to prevent them rising, and pour into the bowl sufficient boiling water to cover the fruit.

The next day halve or quarter the citrons, taking out the pulp carefully (as this being bitter is never used), lay them in your copper preserving-pan, sprinkle a handful of salt over them and cover with cold water. Set the pan on the fire to boil till the fruit is soft enough to pierce with a reed or skewer. Then take the pieces of citron out with a spoon, and put them into very cold water for half an hour, after which squeeze them as dry as you can without breaking. Now put your fruit into the preserving-pan and cover with the sugar, having, after weighing the sugar, measured it out with a cup, as now 4 cups of water to six cups of sugar will be required. Let it melt and boil up slowly with the fruit and set it aside for next day, when it should boil 4 or 5 hours till clear and syrupy, and nice and oily.

This preserve can be candied, but it is kept in jars in syrup, and drained off a few days before it is candied, then rolled in dry sugar, and dried in a cool oven, or on a cake-tray in the sun and air. Green figs are done the same way.

PRESERVE — CITRON
(FROM MY GRANDMOTHER'S RECIPE BOOK. DUTCH)

Scrape the rind, cut citrons in halves, take out the pulp, lay them in a basin of hot water to which a handful of salt was added; change the water the next day, then leave for two days longer in water. After that, boil them in clean water till soft enough to put a reed through. Press all the water out carefully, laying on a cloth to cool. For each pound of fruit take two of sugar; make a syrup of sugar (one cup of water for a cup of sugar), clarify with an egg. Boil for two days on a slow fire. Keep well corked in glass bottles.

PRESERVE — FIG
(OLD CAPE)

To preserve white figs whole, take them nearly ripe, peel thinly, but leave the stalks on; lay for a night in lime water, the next day prick with a needle. Take the weight of the fruit in sugar, make a thick syrup, taking less water than cups of sugar; lay the figs in the syrup, boil gently till the figs are transparent and the syrup thick.

ANOTHER FIG PRESERVE
(FROM A VERY OLD CAPE RECIPE BOOK. DUTCH)

Scrape unripe figs, cut a slit across the top (not *too* large), lay in a basin of cold water in which has been put two tablespoons of lime (this quantity to 100 figs). Lay a plate, with a weight on it, on the top of the figs, or they will drift on the water. About twelve hours after take out, wash clean. Have ready a saucepan in which you have about three quarts of clean water, one teaspoonful of carbonate of soda, one tablespoonful of salt. Let the figs boil up in this, taking care to leave the saucepan *open*. Take out when soft enough to be easily pierced with a reed ; drain through a colander, or on a cloth. Take two pounds of sugar *more* than the weight of fruit, make a clear syrup (one cup of water to one of sugar); then strain and cool, lay your figs in it for a night, the next day preserve on a *slow* fire till the fruit is quite clear. Cork in small jars. Time, three or four hours. *Very good.*

PRESERVE — RIPE FIG

Take six pounds of ripe figs, lay them for a few hours in lime-water (two spoonfuls of lime to a basin of water); take six pounds of sugar, boil a clear syrup; after straining, let it boil till thick before adding the figs; then preserve for two hours longer, slowly, till the figs look clear. Cork. *Will keep well.*

PRESERVING GRAPES (D)

Hanepoot are the best for preserving, and they can be done in the same way as strawberries, but you must prick each grape with a new steel pin before putting them in the jar; fill up with boiling syrup and let it boil in the jars for a few minutes.

PRESERVE — GREEN GRENADILLA (D)

Take 50 grenadillas when the peel is still soft, cut a cross in one end, and scrape or peel very thinly. Take a tablespoon of lime, mix with water; lay the fruit in a deep bowl, cover with this lime water for a night; then another in fresh water. The third day boil in fresh water, to which a tablespoon of salt has been added to make it rather brackish—boiling for 10 minutes, till easily pierced with a reed or straw, and then put them in cold water while preparing the syrup of 6 lb. of sugar to 6 cups of water; boil up and skim. Lay the drained fruit in this, boiling next day till syrup thickens.

PRESERVE — HOTTENTOT FIG OR SOUR FIG

Lay the figs in boiling water till the hard skin is soft and will peel off easily. Take the weight of fruit in sugar, and boil a syrup. Put the fruit (after carefully peeling and cutting off the hard part at the bottom) into the syrup, and preserve *slowly*.

The Hottentot fig is the fruit of a kind of mesembryanthemum which grows wild at the Cape.

PRESERVE — RIPE MELON
(A VERY OLD CAPE RECIPE)

Ingredients:

8 lb. of sugar, boiled with the same quantity of water into a syrup clarified with an egg	6 lb. of melon, ripe 1 oz. of white ginger

Take a large ripe melon (not *too* soft); cut into large slices; prick with a fork, peeling the slices very thinly and removing the seeds. Lay the pieces in a basin, cover with cold water, in which is a teaspoonful of salt, and put a plate on the top to keep the pieces under water. Let it remain in water four or five days; then wash it carefully; put the fruit into boiling water, and let it boil up once; lay the slices of melon on a cloth to drain. Now boil the syrup, and pour it *boiling hot* on the slices of melon, repeating this process every morning for a week; the last two days put the slices of melon in the preserving-pot in which you heat the syrup, and let it boil gently for ten minutes or more, then let it cool. Repeat the next day, and go on till the fruit is quite clear and firm, and the syrup nice and thick. This process diminishes the syrup greatly, and you might add a little more if necessary. This mode of making preserve is rather tedious, but repays one for the trouble; it will keep for years, and becomes beautifully clear and firm. (The ginger to be put in a muslin bag, and boiled with the preserve, and taken out last thing.

PRESERVE — WATERMELON PEEL

Cut the watermelon peel in pieces ; cut off the outer green peel and all the soft inside, cutting away all the red part; then cut into square pieces or shapes, prick well with a fork; lay the pieces in an earthen basin in limewater; leave all night; wash well in cold water next morning; put in some cold water; let peel boil till you can put a stick into it; now drain. Having previously weighed the peel, take the same weight in sugar; set it on the fire in a saucepan, a layer of peel and a layer of sugar, a few sticks of cinnamon, two or three cups of water, close the lid of the stewpan; let it simmer till the sugar is melted, then preserve gently (take the lid off if there is a good quantity of syrup). If the watermelon was an " American Ice-Cream," it will preserve in two or three hours, and be beautifully crisp and soft, almost melting in your mouth. Four or five cloves to be put in the preserve.

PRESERVE — MELON

Made in the same way, only taking *green melons*, while the water-melon should be made from a *ripe one*.

PRESERVE — ICE-CREAM WATERMELON RIND (D)

Take the rind and scoop away most of the red part, but leave a little of this red part on, peel away thinly the hard green outer part, then cut the rind into squares or any fancy shapes. Lay the squares in a bowl and cover with water, into which a small spoonful of lime and a little salt have been stirred, leaving them in it 12 or 14 hours. Then wash them clean and drain.

Rub a very clean copper or enamelled preserving-pot slightly with sweet (Lucca) oil, put the watermelon rind squares, with their weight in sugar, in it and as many cups of water as there are pounds of fruit. Let it come to the boil, and then simmer for 3 or 4 hours with the lid closed.

A good test of when it is done, is to put a little of the syrup on a flat plate; if the syrup is oily and thick enough, little ripples come on the top as it cools. It ought not to sugar, which it will do if boiled too quickly. Bottle it boiling hot, first warming the bottles to prevent cracking, and cork quickly. A nice dessert dish.

PRESERVE — WATERMELON, WITH *DRY* SUGAR

Prick the pieces and lay in lime for a night as for above. Rinse in fresh water in the morning, parboil, putting the peel into water that is *boiling*, drain, but don't squeeze.

To 5 lb. sugar add 6 lb. fruit, while it is still hot, and let it simmer for about half an hour after the sugar is melted. Let it stand for a night, and preserve next day. Test as above.

PRESERVING — WATERMELON PEEL, SPANSPEK PEEL, OR GREEN FIGS WITH *DRY* SUGAR (D)

Pare the figs thinly and cut a cross at the top, or prick the melon peel with a silver fork. Lay in very weak lime water (about a dessert-spoonful to 5 or 6 quarts of water) for one night, next day wash and set to boil in a preserving-pan with cold water (for figs add only a little salt instead of lime to the water). When done so that a thin reed may easily pierce them, take out of the water and put immediately into cold water for 20 minutes. Then take out and drain well, put them in the pan again and strew dry white sugar of the same weight as the fruit over each layer, adding just enough water to moisten the sugar—then cover the pan and set on a slow fire, shaking the pan occasionally until the sugar is dissolved, then let it boil steadily until nearly done, keeping it covered all the time. Remove from the fire, and the next day let it boil again until the syrup is quite thick, when it will crystallize.

PRESERVE — ORANGE, BITTER OR SEVILLE
(MRS. ETHERIDGE'S)

Scrape the rind with a blunt knife or piece of glass. Cut four small incisions at the bottom; put fruit in water for four days, changing the water daily. Boil the oranges until soft, putting them in boiling water. Squeeze them out well. Have ready the syrup—for twelve pounds of fruit eighteen pounds of sugar. Let the oranges lie for a night in syrup before preserving. (Similar to recipe for Nartjiekonfyt).

PRESERVE — PEACHES IN BRANDY
(MRS. H. CLOETE'S)

Ingredients:

150 peaches	2 bottles of white spirits of wine
8 lb. sugar	

The yellow or apricot peaches are generally used. Make a thin syrup of half the sugar (4 lb.). Peel and prick the peaches; boil fifty at a time in the syrup till nearly soft; of the remaining sugar make a very thick syrup. Take three cups of this and two cups of white spirits of wine. Put the preserved peaches in glass jars; pour the mixture over and cork at once.

Should a smaller quantity of peaches be made, the same syrup in which the peaches were boiled might be mixed with the spirits of wine, only boiled till *very* thick.

PRESERVE — WHOLE PEACHES
(MRS. HENRY CLOETE'S OLD CAPE MODE)

Take ripe Clingstone peaches, peel very thinly, prick well. Lay them in a large basin of water to which two spoonfuls of lime have been added (if you have no lime at hand, a handful of kitchen salt will do as well; the effect is to harden the outside of the fruit). Leave the peaches for an hour or two in this. Weigh the fruit before you put it in the limewater ; for twelve pounds of fruit take ten pounds of sugar. Wash the peaches in clean water; oil your preserving pan with olive-oil. Put alternate layers of fruit and sugar, and pour about two or three cups of cold water over; preserve with the lid on the pot for about an hour on rather a quick fire, then let it stew very gently till the syrup looks thick and the fruit looks clear; skim occasionally. Cork when cool. *Will keep well.*

PRESERVING PEARS (D)

The early Saffron pear is most delicious for preserving, and retains its flavour very well. They should be peeled and cored, and if too large to put in in halves, may be cut in four. They should have a thinner syrup than strawberries, as they are very sweet in themselves, and also, being put in the boiling syrup and allowed to boil up once or twice, they absorb more sweetness than the strawberries; the pears must boil for about 8 or 10 minutes till they begin to look clear; fill the jars, as with other fruit, to overflowing, and cork quickly.

PRESERVED PINEAPPLES (D)
(MISS FRANCES CLOETE'S)

Peel and slice the pineapples, and taking the same weight of sugar as the fruit, and a little water, let them preserve in very thin syrup for several hours. A lemon or two squeezed into the preserve shortly before it is done improves it very much.

PRESERVE — QUINCE
(HILDA'S)

Peel and cut the quinces (large ones) in four pieces; carefully core and cut out all the hard inside. Lay in a saucepan, cover with cold water with a handful of salt. Boil quickly till *soft* (for about ten minutes), then drain carefully. The weight of the quinces *after they are peeled* in sugar. Take the peels and cores and pips, cover with cold water, boil well, and strain. Take an equal number of basins of sugar as of the juice. Lay the quinces in a preserving-pan covered with sugar, and the juice of the skins and the cores; preserve gently till the pieces are quite clear, and the juice forms a jelly when cold. This preserve served with whipped cream *is most delicious.*

114

PRESERVE — QUINCE
(MRS. ETHERIDGE'S BOOK)

Peel and cut quinces in thin slices, let them dry a little; the next day preserve in thick syrup, two pounds of sugar more than the weight of the fruit.

PRESERVING STRAWBERRIES (D)

Select sound strawberries of even size, and without stalks. The ripe fruit is put into the jars to fill them, and they are then set in a saucepan with a little water in it, and boiling syrup poured into the jars to cover the fruit. The jars are then brought to the boil in the saucepan, and as the strawberries, being soft, go down, the jars are kept filled up with fruit—then they are corked quickly, wiped and put away; the next morning they are looked over screwed up tightly, and labelled with name of fruit and date.

PRESERVE — TOMATO

Take six pounds of small preserving tomatoes; prick them with a steel pin, and lay them in saltpetre water (a tablespoonful of saltpetre in three quarts of water) for ten minutes. Wash clean; put into a stewing-pan with equal weight of sugar; add half an ounce of dry ginger, just bruised in a mortar and tied in a muslin bag. Let it simmer slowly till the sugar has melted, keeping the preserving-pan closed; then boil rather more quickly for an hour till the tomatoes are clear. Take out ginger before corking the jar.

PRESERVE — TOMATO
(MRS. AHREN'S)

Take middle-sized fruit; prick and cut an incision at the bottom. Lay in lime-water for a night (a tablespoonful of lime in two bottles of water); the next day in a little salt water. Preserve in an equal quantity of sugar. Oil the saucepan, then put in layers of fruit and sugar, alternately, and boil slowly. Half an ounce of ginger in a muslin bag to be added during the boiling, and taken out when done.

PRESERVE — GREEN TOMATOES

Take six pounds of *green*, unripe tomatoes, eight pounds of sugar, boiled to a syrup, and four lemons, the rinds very thinly cut and the juice squeezed.

First boil the tomatoes gently till quite tender, but *don't let them break*. In the water in which the fruit is boiled put about two or three dozen green peach leaves; drain, after taking out. Make a syrup, and put the tomatoes in it cold. Put in two or three pieces of ginger in a bag and the lemon peel; let it boil slowly till quite clear, then take out the ginger. Just before taking the preserve off the fire add about two tablespoonfuls of brandy.

PUDDINGS. — *See also under* Sweets, Chipolata, Chestnut Puddings, Chestnut Snow, Poffertjies, Spritse, Soufflés, Pancakes, Tarts, Pies, Wenteljefies, Junket, Creams, Jellies, Apples, Croquettes, Custards, Dumplings, Fritters, Eggs (Snow), Salads, Omelettes (Sweet), Pears.

PUDDING — ALMOND (D)
(MISS ADEANE'S)

Cover a dish with thin paste; spread raspberry jam at the bottom. Beat up yolks of 8 eggs and the whites of 2. Mix with them ½ lb. powdered sugar, ½ lb. butter, melted and flavoured with almonds (bitter and sweet almonds in equal proportions, well dried and pounded). Mix all well together and pour upon the raspberry jam. Bake the pudding in a slow oven 1½ hours.

PUDDING — ALMOND (D)
(MISS LIESCHING'S)

Ingredients:

1 breakfast-cup of fine bread-crumbs	200 almonds, blanched and minced (or a cup of desiccated cocoanut)
¼ lb. butter	
1 pint milk	1 oz. candied citron
¼ lb. white sugar	1 tsp. ground cinnamon
3 eggs	

First soak the bread in the milk, then beat up the butter, sugar, and yolks of the eggs together; now squeeze the milk out of the bread-crumbs and mix them with the other ingredients and almonds. Whisk the whites stiffly, and add them, beating all the time. Butter a pudding-dish, pour the mixture into it, and bake for three-quarters of an hour, with a buttered paper over the dish.

PUDDING — ALMOND AND RAISIN

Ingredients:

2 oz. beef suet	2 oz. almonds
½ pint milk	3 eggs
¼ lb. bread-crumbs	2 tbsps. rum
½ lb. raisins	2 oz. sugar
A little nutmeg	½ lb. currants

Chop the suet very fine; mix with bread-crumbs, currants, nutmeg and sugar. Butter a mould and line it with raisins, put in rows all round, and almonds blanched and laid between. Beat the eggs, add the milk and rum and mix all together; put carefully in the mould, and boil three hours. Serve with wine sauce.

PUDDING — APPLE

Ingredients:

1 lb. apples	1 lemon
¼ lb. sugar	¼ lb. butter
3 eggs	Puff paste

Pare and core one pound of apples; put them in a stewing-pan, with sufficient water to stew them to a pulp without burning; add sugar, grated rind of lemon, and three well-beaten eggs. Mix all together. Just before baking stir in the butter; line the dish with puff paste and bake three-quarters of an hour. *Very good.*

PUDDING — APRICOT CREAM (D)

Ingredients:

½ lb. dried apricots	1 oz. gelatine
2 oz. lump sugar	2 eggs
½ pint milk	

Soak the apricots 4 or 5 hours, then stew them with sufficient water to cover them, and a little sugar. When quite done, put them through a sieve and let them cool. Then make a custard with the 2 eggs and milk, add the gelatine, and mix all together and put into a mould, set in a cold place, and serve with whipped cream.

PUDDING — BACHELOR'S
(A VERY OLD HOME RECIPE)

Ingredients:

1½ cups of bread-crumbs	½ lb. of sugar
3 oz. of flour	1 tsp. of nutmeg, ginger, and cinna-
4 eggs	mon mixed
½ lb. currants or raisins	1 tsp. of soda
½ lb. of suet	Any candied preserves cut up

Mix all together and add about one pint of buttermilk; if not to be had, use sweet milk, in which case substitute baking-powder for soda. Boil three or four hours. Serve with wine sauce.

PUDDING — BLACKBERRY (D)
(MRS. SMITH'S)

Line a dish with slices of bread and butter, and put a layer of blackberries with lots of sugar, another layer of bread and butter, and so on till the dish is full; bake it for an hour, and serve with custard. Mulberries done this way are very good also.

PUDDING — BAKED BREAD (D)
(OLD GERMAN)

Soak some slices of bread in a pint of milk and three eggs, beaten together. When well moistened fry in a pan with butter. Meanwhile boil in a saucepan a tumbler of light wine, ½ cup of stoned raisins, 25 blanched almonds cut in strips, a cup of sugar and some powdered cinnamon. Boil all this well. Lay the fried bread when ready in a dish, pour the sauce over it, bake to heat thoroughly, and serve hot or cold.

PUDDING — BROWN
(MRS. BURRELL'S)

Two eggs, their weight in flour and butter, the weight of one in sugar. Beat the butter to a cream with sugar; add the eggs well-beaten, stir in the flour, then two tablespoonfuls of jam or fruit jelly; before putting the pudding in a mould, stir in half a teaspoonful of carbonate of soda. Boil or steam for an hour and three-quarters; allow plenty of room for the pudding to rise in the mould. Serve with wine or sweet sauce. Golden syrup may be substituted for jam.

PUDDING — BONNIE'S

Ingredients:

½ lb. of butter, stirred to a cream	3 eggs, yolks and whites separately
¼ lb. sifted sugar	whisked
¼ lb. flour	¼ lb. raisins, split and stoned
Vanilla or lemon essence	

Mix sugar and butter, then the yolks, lastly flour, and whites, and raisins. Boil two hours in a buttered mould. *Very good.*

PUDDING — BEEFSTEAK

Ingredients:

1 lb. flour	Enough water to make into a paste
½ lb. suet	the consistency of ordinary
Pepper, salt	dough
1½ lb. beef steak	

Line a buttered basin with the suet crust, half an inch thick; cut the steaks a quarter of an inch thick, beat them with a kitchen mallet; season with pepper, salt, and a sprinkling of flour; lay them in the basin, interspersed with some fat of the beef, add a glass or less of cold water; cover the top with the remainder of the paste, press well down with the thumb; boil in a floured pudding-cloth for three hours. Turn out carefully on a dish.

Mutton or lamb pudding is done the same way, only add a *tiny* piece of finely shredded onion and parsley.

PUDDING — BREAD AND BUTTER
(FROM A DUTCH FAMILY COOKERY BOOK, OVER ONE HUNDRED YEARS OLD)

Take a small loaf of white bread, cut very thin, and butter each slice, and soak in milk; carefully butter a pudding dish, lay the soaked bread and butter in layers in the dish, sprinkling over each layer some almonds blanched and sliced, some slices of citron preserve, some sugar, and currants, till the dish is nearly full; then whisk up four eggs with a spoonful of rosewater and a quart of boiled milk, and pour into the dish. In the process of baking it may become dry; pour some more milk and egg over it, if all was not required to fill the pudding-dish.

PUDDING — BOILED BUTTERMILK

Ingredients:

1 lb. of flour	2 eggs
1½ pints of buttermilk	1 tsp. of soda
¼ lb. of beef suet	Flavour with essence of almonds
1 tbsp. of butter	

Cut the suet very fine, melt the butter, mix with the suet and flour, beat the eggs, mix all together; don't forget a pinch of salt. Boil for two hours in a cloth or mould. Serve with sweet sauce.

PUDDING — BAKED BUTTERMILK

Melt two ounces of butter in a pie-dish; mix a batter of half a pound of flour and one pint of buttermilk, two eggs, half a teaspoonful of soda; flavour with ginger or almonds; pour into the dish. Bake half an hour. Serve at once with crystallized sugar.

PUDDING — CANARY
(Mrs. J. van der Byl's)

Take three eggs, also the weight of three eggs in sugar and butter, and of two eggs in flour, the rind of a lemon grated. Stir the butter to a cream; add sugar and eggs (well whisked) gradually; dredge in the flour. When mixed thoroughly, pour into a buttered mould. Boil for two hours. Serve with any sweet sauce. *Enough for six people.*

PUDDING — CARAMEL CUSTARD (D)
(Tillypronie)

This quantity is to fill a plain mould which would hold a pint and a half. Use only the finest sugar for burning.

Cook 1 tablespoonful cold water and 4 tablespoonfuls icing or castor sugar quickly for about 10 minutes over the fire in the sugar-boiler, but hardly let it brown. Put it in your plain mould and turn it about quickly, so that before it gets quite cold it may adhere to and glaze the bottom and sides of the mould. Do this in the early morning, that it may be set and cold when wanted.

For your pudding, break six yolks of eggs into a basin and beat, but do not froth them. Have 1½ pints of warm (but not hot) milk in a pan, and a teacupful of cream, and to sweeten it, add a tablespoonful of the same fine sugar to the milk, and flavour with a tablespoonful of orange-flower water, add to the eggs, and give a gentle stir round. Now strain this into the mould you had prepared with the sugar lining, and steam very gently for an hour or longer. When your pudding is ready let it stand aside for five minutes before turning out of the mould. When nearly done have the cover only half on to check the cooling. Should the caramel cream look honey-combed when cut, it shows it has been cooked too fast. If wanted stiff, leave two whites of eggs in with the six yolks.

PUDDING — CARROT
(Cape)

Ingredients:

½ lb. flour	3 eggs
½ lb. grated carrots	Salt
½ lb. sugar	Grated peel of lemon and the juice,
½ lb. beef suet	or essence of lemon

Mince or grate the carrots; chop the suet; whisk the eggs. Mix all together; pack in a mould or basin; boil two or three hours. Serve with a wine sauce. *Enough for eight persons.*

PUDDING — CASTLE

Ingredients:

The weights of four eggs in sugar, flour, butter	4 eggs

Beat the butter to a cream; then add sugar, eggs (well whisked), and flour, a dash of grated nutmeg, and brandy for flavouring. Bake in little tin cups for twenty minutes. This quantity fills six cups. Serve with a wine sauce.

PUDDING — CHEESE
(Mrs. D. Cloete's)

Ingredients:

½ lb. of grated cheese	A little mustard
1 egg, well beaten	1 tsp. of butter, cayenne, pepper,
1 teacupful of milk or cream	salt

Mix all well together. Bake in a buttered dish for twenty minutes. *Enough for four or five persons.*

PUDDING — CHEESE (D)
(Mrs. Deneys's)

Beat the following all well together: ¼ lb. grated cheese, 1 egg, 1 teacup milk, a pat of butter, an eggspoonful of salt and a little cayenne pepper. Put in a small pie-dish, and bake a quarter of an hour.

PUDDING — CHEESE SAVOURY (D)
(Mrs. Pike's)

Ingredients:

½ lb. stale bread-crumbs	A little cayenne pepper
Pepper and salt to taste	A little warm milk
1 egg	A piece of butter, the size of a
4 oz. grated cheese	walnut

Put the cheese, bread-crumbs and seasoning in the dish. Beat up the yolk of the egg with half a teacupful of warm milk, and pour this over the other ingredients, mixing all together in the dish with a fork. Beat the white of the egg to a froth and pour on top of the pudding, lightly mixing in to the top of the other ingredients. Bake for a quarter of a hour in a quick oven.

PUDDING — CHOCOLATE
(German)

Ingredients:

¼ lb. grated chocolate   1 pint of milk
¼ lb. pounded loaf sugar   ¼ lb. of fine flour
¼ lb. butter

Mix all these ingredients and stir into the boiling milk; stir till the substance gets loose from the pot; put it in a dish *to cool.* Then take six eggs; whisk the yolks and whites separately. First add to the mixture the yolks, then, when well stirred, add the whites, well whisked. Put into a buttered porcelain mould; boil one hour; turn out and serve. May be eaten hot or cold.

PUDDING — CITRON
(Klapmuts)

Ingredients:

1 oz. packet gelatine   6 eggs, whisked separately
1 cup light wine   Juice of 3 lemons or oranges
½ lb. white sugar

Dissolve the gelatine (after soaking) in a cup of boiling water. Squeeze the juice of the lemons or oranges, carefully removing the seeds; add the peel of one orange, cut very thin, to the hot water and gelatine, also the juice, one cup of wine, and the sugar. Stir till it comes to the boil Take out the peel; draw aside; pour in the six yolks well whisked. Whip all well together; put into a buttered mould to set.

PUDDING — COCOANUT (D)
(Miss Breda's)

Ingredients:

2 oz. butter   ½ cup bread or stale sponge-cake
½ lb. desiccated cocoanut   crumbs
2 oz. sugar   1 cup milk
4 eggs   ½ tsp. vanilla essence

Cream the butter and add the sugar and the beaten yolks of the egg well whisked, then put in the cocoanut and stir well before adding the milk and the bread-crumbs, and lastly 2 egg-whites whipped to a froth. Pour this mixture into a pie-dish, which should not be quite full, and bake for half an hour. Have ready the other 2 egg-whites whipped to a stiff froth with 1 oz. sifted sugar and ½ teaspoonful of vanilla essence. Pile this in large spoonfuls on the top of the pudding and put it back in the oven, to get slightly brown, for a few minutes. You can decorate the pudding with crystallized cherries or candied citron, before piling on the whisked whites.

ANOTHER (ALSO MISS BREDA'S)

Ingredients:

3 oz. butter	3 oz. crumbs
6 eggs	3 oz. cocoanut

Proceed as in the above recipe, putting on 3 egg-whites at the end and mixing 3 egg-whites in.

PUDDING — COLD WATER (D)
(MISS CARTWRIGHT'S)

Ingredients:

2 oz. fresh butter	1 lemon
3 to 4 eggs	8 tbsps of cold water
¼ lb. sifted sugar	

Beat the butter to a cream; add the yolks of the eggs, then the sugar and water, the juice of the lemon and grated rind; beat the whites of the eggs to a stiff froth to add last, and beat all well together; bake in a slow oven, for half an hour or more, and serve quickly.

PUDDING — CUSTARD
(A FAVOURITE CAPE RECIPE)

Take four eggs; whisk well in an ordinary-sized pie-dish; take either new or boiled milk; add two large spoonfuls of white crystallized sugar, a few drops of vanilla essence. Bake in a moderate oven. A sure way to prevent the custard from becoming watery is to put the pie-dish in a tin with a little water whilst baking. Serve either hot or cold. Can be flavoured with two bay leaves, cinnamon, or vanilla.

PUDDING — DICK'S

Ingredients:

4 oz. bread-crumbs	3 eggs
4 oz. currants	A little cinnamon, and grated nut-
4 oz. apples	meg
2 oz. sugar	

Mince the apples very finely; add currants (well washed), grated bread-crumbs and sugar. Whisk the eggs, and mix all thoroughly. Put the pudding in a buttered basin; tie down with a cloth; boil for three hours. *Sufficient for four or five persons.*

PUDDING — FRUIT

A dish lined with puff paste, and filled with any fruit that is in season, peeled, sliced, and sprinkled with sugar, and baked gently for two or more hours, makes a nice dish served with thin custard, or cream and sugar.

PUDDING — FRUIT (D)
(Mrs. E. Eksteen's)

Boil 1 lb. of any fruit to a pulp—apples, quinces, plums, etc., and sweeten to taste. When cold add a very little butter, and 4 well-beaten eggs. Butter a mould well, and sift into it a thick layer of bread-crumbs, then lay in the fruit, and cover with a half-inch layer of bread-crumbs. Bake for an hour in a moderate oven and turn out when cold.

PUDDING — DATE (D)
(Miss Liesching's)

Ingredients:

1 lb. stoned dates	¼ lb. flour
½ lb. chopped suet	½ cup milk
Salt	1 tsp. mixed ginger and cinnamon
¼ lb. sugar	1 wineglass of brandy
1 cup bread-crumbs	2 eggs

Mix all as you would a plum pudding; pack in a buttered mould; boil for 3 hours. Serve with pudding sauce.

PUDDING — FAIRY CREAM OR ORANGE PUDDING (D)

For this take 1 oz. gelatine soaked in cold, and then dissolved in half a teacup of warm water, 6 oz. sifted or rolled sugar, some grated orange-peel, 1 tumbler white wine, the juice of 6 oranges (strained), 1 breakfast-cup of cream.

The wine, gelatine, and sugar are first boiled together, and the orange-juice added when boiling. It is then removed from the fire. When it is nearly cold, but before it stiffens, add the cream beaten to a stiff froth, and the rind, then pour into a wetted porcelain mould to cool.

PUDDING — FLUMMERY (D)

Yellow Flummery: Take 1 oz. isinglass and dissolve it in a little water, then add 1 pint of sherry wine, the yolks of 4 or 5 eggs, the juice of 2 lemons and sugar to your taste. Let it boil a few minutes then strain it into a basin, and keep stirring till nearly cold. Pour into wet moulds.

White Flummery: Boil 1 oz. isinglass in a little water till quite dissolved, then add 1 pint of cream and 2 tablespoonfuls of brandy. Chop a few bitter and sweet almonds, the peel of 1 lemon, and a little sugar to taste. Boil all a few minutes, then strain through a fine sieve; keep stirring till nearly cold, and pour into wetted moulds.

PUDDING — GINGER
(Mrs. Eksteen's)

Ingredients:

¼ lb. chopped suet
¼ lb. sugar
½ lb. flour

1 egg
1 large tsp. ground ginger
½ cup milk

Stir all well together; boil for 2 hours in a mould. Serve with any fruit sauce or custard.

PUDDING — GUAVA MOULD (D)

Peel, slice and pulp ripe guavas, add a little water and strain out the seeds; you then add 1 cup of sugar to every 3 cups of juice and let it boil well for 5—10 minutes. Some gelatine should meanwhile have been soaked, and you then add ½ packet of soaked gelatine to every 4 cups of the guava. Boil the mixture up again, and pour into a porcelain mould. Serve with cream or custard.

PUDDING — JENNY LIND

Ingredients:

1 lemon
4 eggs
1 breakfast-cup of white wine
¼ pint of cream

½ cup of any kind of preserve, and
    some whipped cream
2 oz. sugar
4 sponge biscuits

Put the juice and grated peel of the lemon into an enamelled saucepan, place over the fire or stove; stir in the well-beaten yolks of four eggs, keep over the fire till nearly boiling. Have ready the whites of four eggs well whisked, stir in the yolks, adding half the breakfast-cup of wine. Put the sponge biscuits into a dish, pour over them the other half-cup of wine; when soaked lay over them some preserve and pour the custard made from the yolks of the eggs and lemon over them, then pile some whipped cream on the top. Ornament it with harlequin comfits. *Very good.*

PUDDING — HASTY (D)
(Mrs. Cox's)

Put a tablespoon flour in a basin, mix with it 1 egg (previously well beaten) and a little milk, to a very smooth paste—no lumps. Then add 1 pint of boiling milk and a pinch of salt, and boil twenty minutes. Must be sent *hot* to the table, and served with treacle.

PUDDING — AN EXCELLENT BAKED LEMON
(Mrs. Etheridge's)

Ingredients:

2 large lemons	6 oz. sugar
3 oz. butter	5 eggs

Take the peel of two large lemons, boil it tender in half a pint of water and pound in a mortar; add the juice and pulp of the lemons carefully taking out the seeds, three ounces of butter stirred in melted, and sugar well beaten up first with the eggs. Line a dish with puff paste, pour in the mixture, and bake for an hour.

PUDDING — LEMON SAGO (D)
(Sister Ryan's, an Army Sister)

Take a teacup of sago and 2 teacups of boiling water. Stir over the fire till clear; if too thick add a little more water. Add the juice of 2 lemons, the grated rind and sweeten with golden syrup. Garnish a mould with slices of lemon, pour in the mixture, and add a layer of slices on top.

PUDDING — LEMON SOLID (D)
(Mrs. Fife's)

Ingredients:

1 lb. lump sugar	$\frac{1}{2}$ pint of milk
1 oz. gelatine	The yolks of 3 eggs
2 lemons	

Dissolve the gelatine in half a pint of boiling water; keep stirring till it is dissolved. Squeeze the lemon juice into the sugar; add the grated rinds of the lemons. Beat the eggs well and add the milk to them, then putting all the ingredients together, stir them well a few moments, and strain through muslin. Put the mixture into a well-wetted mould, and when cold turn out.

All such shapes have the additions of blanched almonds stuck in hedgehog fashion, or whipped cream in the centre of the mould or round the shape. If more colour is desired, a few crystallized cherries, or any other decorative sweetmeat, can be put into the top points of the mould. So good, a friend calls it ambrosia.

PUDDING — MACARONI

Ingredients:

1 lb. macaroni	A wineglass of brandy
1 quart milk	Peel of 1 lemon
4 eggs	2 oz. sugar

Simmer the macaroni in a pint of milk for three-quarters of an hour till quite soft with the lemon-peel; take out the peel, and put the macaroni in a pie-dish lined with puff paste; bend round the edges Beat the eggs well; add sugar and glass of brandy. Stir this into the *other* pint of milk, and pour over the macaroni, and bake for half an hour.

I

PUDDING — MADONNA
(Mrs. D. Cloete's)

Ingredients:

10 oz. bread-crumbs	1 large or 2 small lemons
8 oz. sugar (white or brown)	1 egg
8 oz. beef suet	A tbsp. of brandy

Chop the suet very fine, mix it with the bread-crumbs, sugar, grated lemon-peel; then add the juice, brandy, and egg well beaten. Mix well together with a wooden spoon, and pack firmly into a well-buttered mould. Boil one and a half hours. Serve with sweet or wine sauce.

PUDDING — MANCHESTER
(Mrs. Fleming's)

Boil a pint of milk, pour it boiling over six ounces of bread-crumbs; when nearly cold add two ounces of white sugar. Beat up two ounces of butter and two eggs; butter a pudding-dish, and at the bottom lay a covering of jam; pour mixture over it, and bake in a quick oven for twenty minutes. *Enough for six. As nice hot as cold.*

PUDDING — MOLLY'S

Ingredients:

Stale penny loaf	1 egg
Marmalade	1 pint of milk
1 oz. maizena	

Put a layer of stale bread-crumbs into a buttered dish or basin, then a layer of jam, then another of crumbs, and so on till the dish is full. Then mix a tablespoonful of maizena and one egg, add to it a pint of boiling milk, pour this over the bread-crumbs. Either bake or boil. Time, half an hour. *Cheap and good.*

PUDDING — ORANGE
(Mrs. Fleming's)

Peel six oranges and cut them in small pieces. Make a custard with a pint of milk, two ounces of sugar, two tablespoonfuls of corn-flower, the yolks of two eggs. When nearly cold, pour custard over the oranges, and mix well together. Beat the whites of the eggs to a stiff froth with three spoonfuls of sifted loaf sugar. Heap this on the pudding, and bake in the oven a *light* brown.

126

PUDDING — POTATO
(COPIED FROM OUR GRANDMOTHER'S DUTCH BOOK)

Take a soup-plate of potatoes, boiled and mashed; a spoonful of butter, melted, two tablespoonfuls of fine flour, six eggs, white and yolk whipped separately; about two dozen almonds; a few tablespoonfuls of rose-water. Mix the yolks with the mashed potatoes, then the flour, then the whites of the eggs, the grated almonds, and rose-water. Butter the mould, and garnish with slices of citron preserve, and boil two hours. Can be served with sifted sugar and melted butter, or any sweet sauce.

PUDDING — SWEET POTATO
(CAPE)

Ingredients:

¾ lb. of sweet potatoes, boiled and mashed very fine	3 eggs
	1 tsp. sifted cinnamon
¼ lb. butter	A little nutmeg
¼ lb. loaf sugar	½ wineglass brandy

Stir the butter to a cream with the sugar; whip the eggs separately. Mix all with the mashed sweet potatoes, etc. Line a tart-dish with puff paste; bake for half an hour in a quick oven. When done, sift sugar on the top.

PUDDING — PLUM
(OLD ENGLISH)

Ingredients:

1 lb. raisins	7 eggs
1 lb. currants	2 oz. flour
1 lb. beef suet	1 tbsp. of mixed spices, ginger,
½ lb. candied citron	cinnamon, nutmeg
¾ lb. sugar	1 tumbler of brandy

Stone and clean the raisins, wipe the currants; cut the beef suet very fine, also the candied citron; whisk the whites and yolks separately; mix all together. Boil in a well-floured cloth, or mould, for six hours. Improves by being made weeks before, and kept till wanted. *Very good.*

PUDDING — PLAIN PLUM PUDDING (D)

Ingredients:

4 eggs	¼ lb. flour
1 glass of milk	¼ lb. bread-crumbs
1 wineglass of brandy	¼ lb. mixed peel
½ tsp. salt	½ lb. beef suet
2 oz. almonds	½ lb. sultanas
1 lemon	½ tsp. soda
¼ lb. moist sugar	½ lb. currants

Rub the flour, salt, and suet well together, then add the bread-crumbs, currants, raisins, peel, and sugar, beat up the eggs and stir well, adding the brandy last. Boil in a floured cloth or in a mould for 4 or 5 hours.

PUDDING — RICH PLUM PUDDING (D)
(MRS. BRADY'S)

Ingredients:

½ lb. each of bread-crumbs, raisins, currants, suet, sugar, and chopped apple
¾ lb. almonds
¼ lb. mixed candied peel
½ a grated nutmeg

1 tsp. grated ginger
½ tsp. mixed spice
6 eggs
1 wineglass brandy
1 tsp. salt

Stone the raisins, wash and pick the currants, chop up the suet and apples, crumb or grate the bread, which must be stale, cut up the candied peel fine, whisk the eggs. Mix all thoroughly well together and boil in a buttered mould, tied up in a floured cloth for 6 hours. Serve with a custard. To use up cold remains, squares of this in batter make a nice fritter.

PUDDING — AN EXCELLENT PLUM
(MADE WITHOUT EGGS. ENGLISH)

Ingredients:

½ lb. flour
6 oz. raisins
6 oz. currants
6 oz. chopped suet
¼ lb. brown sugar
¼ lb. mashed potatoes

1 tsp. of mixed spices—ginger, cinnamon, nutmeg
1 tbsp. of treacle or golden syrup
1 oz. candied lemon-peel
1 oz. citron
¼ lb. mashed carrots

Mix flour, currants, suet, sugar, well. Have ready the above proportions of carrot and potato, and stir them into the other ingredients add treacle and lemon-peel, but no other liquid, *or it will be spoiled.* Boil in a mould, but do not fill it quite, as it must have room to swell. Let it boil for four hours. This pudding is best mixed overnight. Serve with brandy sauce. (*See* Sauce for Puddings, " Bessie's.")

PUDDING — PLAIN, GOOD

Ingredients:

1 quart boiled milk
¼ lb. mashed potatoes
¼ lb. flour

2 oz. butter
2 oz. sugar

Mix the ingredients, and when cold, add 3 well-beaten eggs; flavour with essence of bitter almonds or vanilla. Bake or steam for half an hour. Serve with wine sauce. (*See* Bessie's Recipe among Sauces for Puddings.)

PUDDING — POMMES À LA RUSSE (D)

Ingredients:

Apples	Sugar
Mincemeat	Water

Take any kind of stewing or dessert apple, peel and core well; fill the centre with mincemeat, made as for mince pies; have ready a syrup made of a cup of sugar to a cup of water. When boiling, put in the apples and boil till clear; take care that the syrup only comes up to the apples and does not cover. May be eaten hot or cold.

PUDDING — QUEEN OF PUDDINGS
(MRS. HENRY CLOETE'S)

Take the crumb of a penny loaf of white bread, *well* soaked in boiling milk; whisk the yolks of three eggs; a good tablespoonful of butter, lemon-peel or cinnamon. Mix all. Bake in the oven. When nearly cold, put on a layer of apricot jam, or gooseberry. Whisk the whites to a stiff froth with one cup of sifted sugar and the juice of a lemon ; cover the preserve. Put back in the oven to dry—*not brown.*

PUDDING — QUINCE

Ingredients:

7 quinces	Powdered ginger, cinnamon
1 pint cream	½ lb. sugar
4 eggs	Puff paste

Boil seven large quinces until *very* tender, pare and core them; beat to a pulp, adding the sugar. Beat up the eggs, stir gradually into a pint of cream; mix with the pulp; flavour with cinnamon or ginger; put into a buttered dish with puff paste round. Bake for three-quarters of an hour. Serve with sugar.

PUDDING — RICE
(OLD DUTCH, MRS. MYBURGH'S)

Ingredients:

5 tbsps. of pounded rice	8 oz. of sugar
1 quart of milk	2 oz. of butter
6 eggs	1 tsp. of cinnamon

Boil the rice and milk till thick and soft. Let it *cool;* stir in the butter; whisk whites and yolks separately, mix with the rice and milk. Bake three-quarters of an hour in a buttered mould dusted with fine biscuit. Turn out when cold.

PUDDING — RICE
(MY MOTHER'S)

Boil one cupful of rice in one and a half quarts of new milk; when soft stir in a tablespoonful of butter. When cold, whisk up three eggs, add cinnamon or Nartjie (Tangerine orange) peel, stir well together, and bake for twenty minutes in a buttered pie-dish. *Very good.*

129

1*

PUDDING — RICE CREAM AND APRICOTS (D)

Ingredients:

½ lb. rice	Milk
Isinglass	Lemon-peel
Sugar	Canned apricots

Wash, dry, and pound the rice. Boil it in a pint of new milk with a little isinglass, lemon-peel, and sugar. When nearly cold mix with half a pint of thick cream whipped. Pour it into a ring mould to set. Turn out, and put the apricots in the centre. *Very good.*

PUDDING — ROLY-POLY JAM
(MY MOTHER'S)

Ingredients:

1 lb. flour	Eggspoonful of salt
½ lb. of finely cut beef suet	1 pint of cold water

Mix all well together, roll out *very thinly.* Leaving a small edge of half an inch for the dough to stick, cover the whole surface with jam (will take about three-quarters of a pound—quince jam is very good), roll up, fasten the ends well; have ready a cloth which has been dipped in boiling water and well dusted with flour; put the roly-poly in this; tie up the ends well, putting a little dry flour at each end of the cloth, to prevent the water getting in. Put into boiling water, and let it boil for two or three hours.

PUDDING — POTATO ROLY-POLY
(ENGLISH)

Take a pint of hot mashed potato, a pint of flour, a quarter of a pound of butter, a pinch of salt, and moisten with milk or water to a dough. Roll the paste out, spread it with any jam that has no stones, roll and tie up, and steam for an hour and a quarter. A very nice sauce to eat with this dainty pudding, is, two ounces of butter and two tablespoonfuls of sugar beaten together, and added to one well-beaten egg; go on beating, pouring in by degrees a little boiling water till the sauce looks like cream.

PUDDING — ROMAN
(A NICE RECIPE FOR COLD MEAT)

Mince some cold meat—veal, chicken, or beef; take a cup of good stock, nicely flavoured, one egg, a little vermicelli or bread-crumbs, pepper, and salt; mix all together, with a suspicion of onion and parsley. Line a meat mould or basin with some macaroni, previously boiled quite tender in milk or water, then fill with the mincemeat. Steam for half an hour; if made of uncooked meat it should steam for an hour and a half. When done, turn out of the basin. Serve with a nice white sauce. *Makes a nice entrée.*

PUDDING — SAGO AND PONTAC (D)
(Mrs. Clayton's)

Take a cupful of sago and boil in sufficient water to make it clear. Sweeten with a cup of sugar and stir in a glass of pontac. Put in a mould to cool.

PUDDING — SNOW (D)
(Mrs. Eksteen's)

Ingredients:

Half a packet of gelatine
A small teacupful of sugar
The whites of 3 eggs

The juice of 3 lemons
Lemon essence

Cover the gelatine with cold water and let it soak for half an hour. Then pour over it one pint of boiling water and stir till melted, now add the sugar and stir awhile till dissolved, then add the juice of the lemons, and a little lemon essence. Stir all together and let it set. When quite cold, beat the mixture till it looks like snow. Beat the whites of the eggs stiff, and stir into the mixture. Place in a wetted porcelain mould. Make a rich custard of the yolks of the eggs to serve with it.

PUDDING — SCHAUM, FOAM OR BESSIE'S

Ingredients:

3 tbsps. of maizena
3 eggs
2 tbsps. of sugar
3 breakfast-cups of milk
A dessertsp. of butter

A tiny pinch of salt
1 tsp. of vanilla essence or a bit of cinnamon, or 10 drops of essence of almonds

Set the milk to boil with the sugar, keeping half a cup to mix with the maizena and butter and yolks of the eggs. When the milk boils, pour in the maizena, etc.; stir till quite done, which can be told by the maizena coming off the bottom of the saucepan. Have ready the whites stirred to a stiff froth, draw the saucepan to the side; let the whites lie on the boiling mixture for a minute or two before stirring it *lightly* with the pudding, then pour into a wetted mould; turn out when cold. Serve with preserved peaches, or very good without. *A very good cold pudding.*

PUDDING — SOUFFLÉ MILAN (D)

Ingredients:

Juice of 6 lemons
6 oz. sugar
1 glass of wine or liqueur

Yolks of 6 eggs
$\frac{1}{2}$ oz. isinglass, dissolved in water

Take the eggs, sugar and lemon-juice and put on the fire stirring till they boil; take them off and add the isinglass and liqueur. Let it cool. Beat the whites of the eggs up, then mix all together and put in a glass dish, adding bruised pistachio nuts. Then ice it.

131

PUDDING — STONE CREAM (D)
(Miss Elliot's)

Put at the bottom of a glass dish 3 spoonfuls of lemon-juice with a little of the peel grated and some apricot sweetmeat, chopped small. Then take 1 pint of rich cream with $\frac{1}{4}$ oz. isinglass dissolved in two-thirds of a pint of water, and sugar to your taste. Let it boil 5 minutes, stirring it all the time; strain it into a jug with a spout or lip, and when the cream is almost cold pour it over the apricot, pouring round and round the dish till all is in. You may ornament the cream with what sweetmeat you please.

PUDDING — ST. LUCIA, EGGLESS (D)

Ingredients:

1 teacup flour	1 small cup Scotch marmalade or
1 teacup bread-crumbs	apricot jam
1 small cup minced suet	1 tsp. salt
1 cup milk	1 large tbsp. baking-powder

Mix the baking-powder with the flour, then add in all the ingredients mixed well, and lastly the milk. Boil in a greased bowl three hours. Serve with a good pudding sauce.

PUDDING — THICK MILK

Ingredients:

$\frac{1}{4}$ lb. fine flour	$\frac{1}{2}$ tsp. soda
Cup fine bread-crumbs	1 wineglass brandy
1 oz. melted butter	1 tbsp. of any jam you fancy
1 egg, whisked	

Mix all, adding a breakfast-cupful of thick milk (as much as would make it the consistency of butter) and boil in a mould for two hours. Serve with a pudding sauce.

PUDDING — THICK MILK, No. 2 (D)
(Miss Breda's)

ngredients:

4 eggs	1 teacup thick milk
4 tbsps. flour	$\frac{1}{4}$ lb. butter
$\frac{1}{4}$ lb. white sugar	

Beat eggs separately, mix yolks with sugar and butter, then flour and sour milk, lastly add the whites; boil in a mould for two hours, serve with cinnamon and sugar, or a pudding sauce.

PUDDING — TAPIOCA

Soak two tablespoonfuls cf tapioca in a quart of milk for four hours, then set it on the fire with two ounces of sugar and a little grated lemon-peel. When clear pour it into a pudding-dish; whip up two eggs well, mix with the tapioca and milk. Bake half an hour. *Excellent.*

PUDDING — TOMATO AND MEAT
(Mrs. Fleming's)

Cover the bottom of a dish with bread-crumbs, put on this a layer of underdone meat cut in thin strips, sprinkled with pepper, salt, and a little onion, then a layer of ripe tomatoes peeled and sliced, an even teaspoonful of brown sugar, a few pats of butter. Repeat this till the dish is full, lastly a layer of bread-crumbs. Bake a nice brown. The meat can be minced if preferred.

PUDDING — YORKSHIRE
(To eat with roast beef)

Ingredients:

2 eggs	3 tbsps. of flour
1 pint milk	Salt

Mix all together; either bake in a pan or under the roast. Time, half an hour. If eggs are scarce, chop up two ounces of suet, and mix as above, and bake in the same way. This pudding should be made flat and cut in squares.

PUFF PASTE

Roll about a quarter of a pound of butter into one and a half pounds of flour, with the juice of half a lemon; mix with thin cream instead of water; add the yolk and white of one egg; a little water may be added if necessary. Roll out thinly and put the butter on in little dabs; roll out again and spread the rest of the butter, fold it up and let it lie for an hour, then use for tarts or savoury pies. This quantity would make the crust for a large pie, two or three tarts, etc. Can safely be made the day before it is wanted in cool weather.

PUNCH — MILK
(Admiral Etheridge's, Madras)

Ingredients:

12 oranges	5 bottles of brandy
12 limes	6 quarts water
Peel and juice	6 lb. sugar
4 bottles of rum	4 quarts boiling milk

Put the peel of the oranges and limes on the brandy for three days. Then mix the sugar and three quarts of lime and orange-juice well together, stir with the brandy till all the sugar is dissolved. Take out the peel and add six quarts of water, and lastly pour in four quarts of boiling milk, stir, and cover up for a couple of hours; then strain through a double flannel till quite clear. Bottle for use. Be careful that the milk is boiling.

PUFFS — BOSTON
(A NICE TEA CAKE)

Ingredients:

4 oz. of butter	½ lb. of flour
6 or 3 eggs	½ pint of water

Put water in a saucepan, add butter, boil slowly. Stir in gradually the flour, beating well, then boil a few minutes. Turn out to cool, beat in the yolks of the eggs, and last the whites, beaten to a stiff froth. Drop from a spoon on sheets of greased paper laid up on a pan or tin, in a hot oven for twenty minutes. When baked, slit open and fill with some jam; serve hot.

Q

QUAILS

Quails are very plentiful at the Cape in October and November. They are generally cooked in a baking-pot—the old Dutch way. Cut off the wings at the first pinion, leaving the feet; pass a skewer through the pinions and wings; cover the breast with a young vine leaf and a slice of fat bacon. Bake a nice brown. Serve on buttered toast, with good gravy poured on them. Bread sauce can be served with them.

Note.—In some Cape houses *curried* quail is considered a great delicacy.

QUAIL.—*See* Pie, A luxurious Quail.

QUINCE SAMBAL — GREEN CHUTNEY
(MALAY)

Take two or three greenish quinces; peel and quarter them; a few slices of onion, a green chilli, and some salt. Pound all these in a mortar, and serve with roast or curry. *A very good condiment.*

R

RAGOUT OF COLD DUCK OR TURKEY
(MALAY OR CAPE DISH)

Cut up the remains of cold duck, etc.; make a little stock of the bones; flavour with cayenne pepper, mustard, tomato sauce. Cut a large onion into small pieces; fry (or " smoor " as they say in Dutch) in boiling fat or butter. Mix with the stock, which can be thickened with a little brown flour. When this mixture is broiling, add your pieces of cold duck, turkey, or chicken. After being slightly browned, pour the savoury mixture over them, and let the whole simmer for a quarter of an hour till thoroughly warm.

RAGOUT — TONGUE
(Miss Becker's, German)

Boil a fresh tongue for two or three hours, with two dozen whole peppercorns, a small piece of ginger (pounded), two bay leaves, a spoonful of salt. When nice and soft, take out peel and cut in thin slices. Then take a quarter of a pound of butter, two spoonfuls of flour; stir with the butter over the fire till nice and brown; stir in a cup of the soup that the tongue has been boiled in, one glass of madeira, some cayenne pepper, some potted mushrooms. Simmer the tongue in this mixture for a few minutes. Serve with croquettes of minced meat, nicely seasoned, rolled in bread-crumbs, and fried in a pan in boiling fat. Garnish with small potatoes, boiled in their jackets, then *peeled* and fried in bread-crumbs and lard. *A very nice entrée.*

RIBS OF BEEF — SPICED BONED
(Home Recipe)

For ten pounds of beef, take a breakfast-cup of salt, two table-spoonfuls of sugar, a full teaspoonful of saltpetre, about twenty-four cloves, twenty-four allspice, a teaspoonful of pepper, bruised and well rubbed into the beef. Bone, roll and skewer the beef, and leave in the pickle for a week. Steam for three or four hours, and place between plates with weights on it to press it firmly together. *Excellent—to be eaten cold.*

RICE — BOILED
(Cape)

Ingredients:

1 pint of rice	2 quarts of water

Wash the rice three times, then put it into two quarts of boiling water with a teaspoonful of salt. Let it boil briskly till the rice is soft, then drain off all the water by putting the rice in a colander; pour a pint of cold water over the rice when in the colander; put it back in the saucepan, and set it on the stove till it is quite dry, and each grain of rice separate from the other. Time, half an hour. *Enough for curry for six people.*

RICE — YELLOW
(Malay)

Ingredients:

1 pint of rice	1 tbsp. of butter
2 quarts of water	1 tsp. of pounded turmeric
¼ lb. of light yellow sugar	Some sultana raisins or currants

Wash the rice well; set it on the fire with two quarts of water and all the ingredients at once. Let it boil for half an hour. *A very favourite dish with Cape children.*

RICE MILK
(A HOMELY DISH)

Put a quart of milk into a pie-dish; take half a pint of rice, wash and crush slightly, and put into the milk; set the dish in the oven with a tin plate over it to prevent scorching. Serve with sugar. Tapioca done in the same way is very good.

RICE AND TOMATOES (D)

Cook some tomatoes, cut in half carefully, scoop out the soft inside, mix with boiled rice, so that it looks pink. Fill the tomato skins with forcemeat with a good deal of truffle in it, and lay on top of a flat dish of the pink rice.

RISSOLES.— *See also* Frikkadel.

RISSOLES OR CROQUETTES
(MRS. FLEMING'S)

Mince finely about one and a half pounds of cold meat—cold roast beef, fowl or veal is best; also a few slices of ham, raw or boiled; season with salt, white pepper, nutmeg, a *very* tiny shred of onion chopped to *powder*, and a little chopped parsley. Put two ounces of butter into a stew pan; when melted stir in gradually a large table-spoon of flour; then add a teacupful of milk and the same quantity of stock. When this is sufficiently cooked to take away the rawness of the flour, stir in the meat, adding two tablespoonfuls of bread-crumbs, three eggs lightly beaten, a little catsup, tomato sauce, or Worcestershire sauce, and, if liked, a little grated lemon-peel. Stir all this for a few minutes in the stew-pan, then set it to cool before shaping into balls (which can be nicely formed by pressing them in a wineglass) or into rolls slightened flattened; dip them in egg and roll in crumbs after being formed. Then you put into a saucepan as much lard as when melted would cover them; and when the lard boils, drop the rissoles in, and let them get a golden brown. The lard can be used again and again. *Very good.*

RISSOLES — FISH
(AN OLD DUTCH WAY)

Ingredients:

1 lb. of fish	Some nutmeg
1 onion fried in butter	A little cayenne
1 good slice of soaked bread squeezed very dry	A little salt
Some parsley	2 eggs

Mince the fish very fine; mix with squeezed bread, flavouring, and egg, and dust a little *dry biscuit* into it as you are rolling it into shapes; roll in egg and fine bread-crumbs or dry biscuit pounded, and fry in lard. Serve in a hot dish, with a little melted butter and tomato sauce. *Very good.*

ROLLS — HOT

Ingredients:

    2 lb. of flour   A little salt
    A tsp. of soda

Mix the soda and salt well with the flour; then mix with butter-milk or sour milk into the consistency of ordinary dough. Cut with a knife into little rolls. Bake half an hour in a quick oven or baking-pot. *For a dozen people.*

ROUND OF BEEF — SPICED
(MRS. FITZPATRICK'S)

Ingredients:

24 lb. of round of beef	1 oz. of nutmeg
3 oz. of saltpetre	$\frac{1}{2}$ oz. of allspice
3 oz. of coarse black sugar	3 handfuls of coarse salt
1 oz. of cloves	

Pound all the ingredients except the meat finely together; rub in to the beef twice a day, turning it each time, for fifteen days; put into a pan so as to be covered with the pickle liquor formed by the salt, etc., and cover the pan with a cloth. The bone must be taken out, and the meat hung for twelve hours to make it tender. When it is to be dressed, dip it into water to take off the loose spice, and bind it round with tape. Put it into a large pot, with a teacupful of water at the bottom; cover the top of the meat with shred suet, a brown crust, and paper over the whole. Bake for five or six hours. The gravy can be kept for flavouring soup or hash. *Very good. (See also* Beef (Spiced), Mrs. Cloete's Recipe.)

ROASTS.—*See* Beef à la Mode, Beef (Spiced), Beefsteak, Fowls, Gesmoorde Hoender, Lamb, Mutton Chops, Pies, Puddings (Beefsteak), Pudding (Tomato and Meat), Saddle of Mutton, Turkey, Veal, Venison.

S

SADDLE OF MUTTON

The best joint at the Cape is a twelve pound saddle of mutton. When hung for four days it is most beautifully tender, resembling Welsh mutton. Wash and wipe dry; dust with flour, salt, and pepper, and put into a baking-pan in a hot stove oven for two hours, basting occasionally. Serve with quince or red currant jelly.

SALAD DRESSING
(Mrs. Spence's)

Ingredients:

2 hard-boiled eggs	1 tbsp. vinegar
1 dessertsp. dry mustard	2 tbsps. oil
1 tsp. salt	½ cup cream
1 tsp. of brown sugar	

Crush the yolks of the eggs very fine with a tablespoon, in a basin or soup-plate, with the mustard and other dry ingredients; add the oil, little by little, till it is well mixed, then the vinegar, and lastly the cream. This sauce will keep for a week if kept corked in a cool place.

SALAD DRESSING — ANOTHER

Ingredients:

1 cold boiled potato	A little pepper
1 hard-boiled egg yolk	Rather more than a tbsp. of oil
1 tsp. dry mustard	2 tbsps. vinegar
1 tsp. sugar	The white of egg, chopped fine
½ tsp. salt	

Mix like the preceding, and add a little anchovy sauce, if liked.

SALAD — CHICKEN

Ingredients:

Cold fowl	2 tsps. of mustard
2 white-heart lettuces	1 tsp. of sugar
2 dessertsps. melted butter, or salad oil	2 tbsps. vinegar
2 hard-boiled eggs	1 tbsp. cream

Wash and dry the lettuces, reserving centre leaves; cut them fine, lay them at the bottom of the dish. Mince all the white meat from a boiled chicken or fowl (without the skin), and place it on the lettuce. Rub the yolks of two hard-boiled eggs to a smooth paste with the melted butter, or oil, add to it the teaspoonful of mustard, sugar, salt, pepper, and stir gradually with the vinegar—this makes the dressing. Arrange the centre leaves of the lettuce as a border, and the white of eggs, and some small delicate cress, beetroot cut in shapes, or tomato, and when *ready* to serve, pour over the chicken the salad dressing. *A nice Supper or Lunch dish.*

SALAD — CUCUMBER

Ingredients:

Cucumber	Cayenne, or pepper
Spring onion	Lucca oil

Cut the cucumber in very thin slices across, a few slices of spring onion, two spoonfuls of vinegar, a dash of pepper, olive-oil, and, just before serving, a little salt.

SALAD — FRUIT (D)

A nice fruit salad is of oranges, sliced and the pips taken out, with stewed dates, and a syrup of orange-juice over all.

Another good fruit salad consists of layers of pineapples, banana and oranges sprinkled with sugar, with half a wineglass of Van der Hum poured over them.

SALAD — GUAVA, OR ANGEL'S FOOD
(A FAVOURITE CAPE DISH)

Ingredients:

1½ doz. guavas	Sugar
2 oranges	1 glass sherry

Peel and slice the guavas thinly, lay them on a glass dish, sprinkle a little sugar; then a layer of oranges sprinkled with sugar; again guavas, and so on till the dish is filled. Pour over all a glass of sherry. Let it stand for a while. *It is a delicious dessert dish.*

SALAD — FISH, COLD
(MISS BREDA'S, OLD DUTCH)

Take some boiled fish, put a layer of it in a pie-dish or salad-bowl; have ready some raw onion, finely cut, sprinkle a little salt over it; pour hot water on the same to take off the raw taste, and drain immediately; then put a layer of onion between each layer of fish, and also on the top, add a few coriander seeds, pepper and salt to taste, and some vinegar. Let it remain until next day before using.

SALAD — INDIAN CORN (D)

To one tin of Indian corn add 2 tablespoonfuls of mayonnaise sauce, half a pint of whipped cream, pepper and salt to taste, and sufficient aspic to set it. Line a mould with the aspic jelly, and fill it with the mixture. Turn out when cold. Peas, or mixed vegetables could be done in this way too.

SALAD — LOBSTER

Ingredients:

1 lobster	A taste of chilli vinegar
Yolks of 2 eggs	2 tbsps. of salad oil
1 tsp. of mustard	Some fresh lettuces
4 tbsps. of plain vinegar	Some cayenne

Pick all the meat out of a lobster; beat well the yolks of two new-laid eggs, beat in some made mustard, and, continuing to beat, drop in the salad oil; add any flavouring that may be preferred, a taste of chilli vinegar, some plain vinegar (four tablespoons), and the soft part of the lobster. Moisten the remainder of the lobster with this sauce, and lay it at the bottom of the bowl. Cut up the lettuce, rolling it in the dressing, and put it over the lobster.

SALAD — ORANGE

Ingredients:

8 oranges	1 wineglass of brandy
1 pineapple	4 oz. sugar

Peel and core the oranges; lay in a glass dish well sprinkled with sugar, with slices of pineapple between, cut thin, with the rough outside cut off; then add a large wineglass of brandy or sherry. Keep the dish closed for an hour. *Delicious.*

SALSAFY AS AN ENTRÉE

Clean and scrape the salsafy, boil tender, and cut in rounds. Add a white sauce made thus: one ounce of flour, half an ounce of butter, a little milk. Butter an oyster scallop, sprinkle with bread-crumbs, and bake a light brown.

SANDWICHES — PLAIN MEAT

Cut very thin slices of bread and butter from a square loaf baked in a tin, and place very thin slices of tongue, ham, biltong, or game between them; season with salt and mustard or pepper; press them on a board with the blade of a large knife. Cut the crust off evenly and divide them into oblong squares.

SANDWICHES — EGG

Two or three hard-boiled eggs, mashed very finely, and mixed with half an ounce of butter, some pepper and salt. Spread liberally on the bread and butter (cut as for ordinary sandwiches), with a sprinkling of water-cress (cut small) or mustard and cress. The eggs may be also be cut thinly and laid between the bread and butter, with pepper and salt, and cress.

SANDWICHES — SAVOURY

Very savoury sandwiches may be made of bloater paste (see that recipe), and boned anchovies and hard-boiled eggs.

SANDWICHES — VICTORIA
(MRS. DWYER'S)

Ingredients:

4 eggs	The weight of the eggs in butter
A little salt	Pounded sugar, and flour

Beat the butter to a cream, dredge in the flour and pounded sugar; stir these well together and add the eggs, first well whisked. Beat the mixture for ten minutes. Butter a Yorkshire-pudding tin; pour in the batter and bake in a moderate oven for twenty minutes. Let it cool. Spread one-half the cake with any jam or preserve, place over it the other half, press together, and cut in long finger strips. Pile them in cross-bars on a dish and serve.

SASATIES OR KABABS
(Mrs. J. Cloete's, Indian)

Take the thick part of a leg of mutton, cut into small square bits with fat between; put into a large earthenware bowl. Mince a raw onion and some lemon leaves, add a tablespoonful of brown sugar, half a cupful of milk, mix all well together and pour over the meat. Now take two or three onions, cut small, fry in a pan in a spoonful of butter or fat to a nice brown. Take an ounce of tamarinds, pour over it a cup of boiling water; when all the strength has gone out of it, strain and mix with the onions and let it *boil;* then add two spoonfuls of good curry-powder or Indian curry-paste (a clove of garlic, if liked —chopped up) some salt; mix well together, and pour over the meat. The next morning put the meat on skewers, fat and lean alternately. Carefully take all the sauce, put it in a saucepan, and boil with a pat of butter. Roast the skewered meat (sasaties) on a *gridiron* heated on wood coals, and serve with the sauce. Add *chutney* if liked.

SASATIES OR KABABS
(A Malay or Indian Dish, My own)

Ingredients:

1 fat leg of mutton	A tbsp. of sugar
2 oz. of good curry-powder	A cup of milk
½ cup of vinegar, or the juice of 3 lemons (if not to be had, 1 oz. of tamarind drawn on a cup of water gives a very pleasant acid	½ dozen lemon or orange leaves
	2 oz. of butter
	3 doz. skewers, cut out of a bamboo, or iron skewers
	Salt to be added when skewered

Cut up the leg of mutton in little pieces an inch square, brown the onion, cut in thin slices, and fried in a pan in fat or butter. Mix all the ingredients well up with the cut up meat in a deep pan or basin; leave it for a night or longer, and when wanted, place the meat interspersed with fat here and there on the skewers. Place the gridiron on wood coals to get very hot, then grill the sasaties a nice brown. Serve *hot* with rice. The gravy to be heated in a sauce pan, and serve with the sasaties. *A very favourite picnic dish at the Cape.*

SASATIES.— *See also* Bobotie and Curry.

SAUCE — APPLE SAUCE (D)
(For roast pork or duck)

Stew 8 or 10 peeled and cored cooking apples in sufficient water to moisten them, to a pulp. Add ½ oz. butter, 1 oz. sugar and 1 oz. salt. For exact quantity be guided by taste—according to size of apples.

SAUCE — BREAD
(My Mother's)

Ingredients:

1 pint of milk	A small onion
A cup of crumbled crumb of bread	A blade of mace
1 tsp. of butter	A little pepper and salt

Peel and cut the onion in quarters; simmer in the milk till tender; then take out. Stir the fine bread-crumbs into the boiling milk; beat it with a fork very smoothly. Add the seasoning and butter and a little white pepper. Give one more boil. To enrich the sauce a spoonful of cream may be added. Time altogether, half an hour. Serve with turkey, chickens, partridge, etc.

SAUCE — BUTTER, MELTED, FOR FISH, ETC.

Mix the proportions of a teaspoonful of flour to two ounces of butter. Rub the flour and butter in a saucepan; add two tablespoonfuls boiling water, or milk, which is better than water, and if milk is used, less butter is required.

SAUCE — CAPER, FOR BOILED MUTTON

Add a few spoonfuls of capers to a good white sauce.

SAUCE — CELERY, FOR BOILED CHICKEN

Three or four heads of celery boiled in water and a little salt, mashed, and added to any white sauce.

SAUCE — CURRANT, FOR VENISON (D)
(Miss Meinertzhagen's old Recipe)

Boil one ounce of currants in half a pint of water a few minutes; then add a small teacupful of bread-crumbs, 6 cloves, and a glass of port wine, also a bit of butter. Stir till the whole is smooth.

SAUCE — CUSTARD, FOR TARTS AND PUDDINGS

Ingredients:

1 pint of milk	2 spoonfuls of sugar
2 eggs	A spoonful of brandy

Stir two well-beaten eggs into a pint of hot milk and pounded sugar—sweeten to taste—in a jug. Set the jug in a saucepan of boiling water, stir till the consistency of thick cream. Serve over puddings or handed round in a sauce-boat. Care must be taken *not to let it boil.*

SAUCE FOR DEVILLED CHICKEN

Ingredients:

4 tbsps. of cold gravy
1 tbsp. chutney paste
1 tbsp. ketchup
2 tsps. mustard

2 tsps. salt
1 tsp. of butter
A pinch of sugar

Mix all these ingredients as smooth as possible; warm well. Brown your cold meat in a little butter; then add to the mixture and simmer for a few minutes.

SAUCE — DUTCH, FOR FISH
(MRS. KOTZE'S)

Ingredients:

A tbsp. of tarragon vinegar (or the thin liquid of tomato sauce when bottled, the upper part will become quite clear)

The yolks of 2 or 3 eggs
2 oz. of butter
Some salt
A tbsp. of cream

Whip up the yolks in a small saucepan with the vinegar. Keep stirring over the fire till the consistency of rich custard. *Don't let it boil.* Then take the butter and stir that in on the fire; keep stirring all the time. Lastly, add the cream. Time, about six or seven minutes. Must be served *at once.*

SAUCE FOR FLAT FISH — QUIN'S SAUCE (D)

Ingredients:

2 heads of garlic, each clove cut in half

2 sps. of Indian soy
2 sps. of walnut pickle

All to be mixed in one pint of vinegar. Shake well and cork it. N.B.—It will be fit for use in a month, and will keep good for years.

SAUCE — EXCELLENT FOR FISH
(MRS. DWYER'S)

Ingredients:

¼ cup cream
1 tsp. of flour
1 tsp. of anchovy essence
A little chilli vinegar

A little soy
A very little cayenne pepper
A piece of butter, the size of a walnut

Rub the flour and butter together; set it on the fire with the cream, stirring well till boiled, for three or four minutes; then add anchovy, chilli vinegar, a few drops of soy, and a pinch of cayenne.

SAUCE FOR FILLETS DE ROMANO (D)

One cup of any good stock, the yolks of two eggs; a little pepper, salt, cayenne, a tablespoon of tarragon vinegar, a little lemon-juice and some chopped parsley, all well mixed. Let the stock boil, beat up the yolks with some lemon-juice and add to the boiling stock as you would make thin custard.

SAUCE FOR FOWL — COLD BOILED
(Mrs. Spence's)

Ingredients:

1 pint new milk
2 oz. butter
The yolks of 2 eggs
2 oz. maizena

A little salt
A pinch of cayenne
A few strips of lemon-peel, and juice

Mix the maizena, salt, cayenne, and the eggs with a little of the new milk. Boil the rest of the milk, then add the maizena, etc., to it, stirring over the fire till smooth and thick. Pour out and stir till cold; Pour over the fowl. It should lie on it without dropping off. *Very good.*

SAUCE FOR FOWL — COLD BOILED, ANOTHER
(Mrs. Spence's)

Boil your two chickens in a cloth; then take the feet and neck, put into a stew-pan with a cup or more of water, a small blade of mace, a slice of onion. When well boiled, strain through a sieve. Take one cup of this stock, thicken with two ounces of maizena, add a cupful of cream, yolk of an egg, a little cayenne and white pepper. Let it cool, pour over the chicken. Garnish the dish with hard-boiled eggs, cut in slices, beetroot, pieces of carrot. *A very nice dish for lunch or supper.*

SAUCE — FOR HASHED BEEF, VENISON, MUTTON, OR WILDFOWL HASH (D)

Ingredients:

1 pint clear good gravy
1 tbsp. onion, chopped very fine
A little cayenne

A pinch of salt
2 tbsps. mushroom ketchup

Boil these and when boiling put in the meat, cut very thin; turn it 3 or 4 times, and in 4 or 5 minutes send to table to be eaten immediately. *Must not stand.*

SAUCE — FOR HERRINGS, OR SALMON (D)

Tarragon, chervil, parsley and shallots, all chopped fine; add oil and vinegar for herrings. For salmon add a little lemon-juice and cayenne.

SAUCE — HORSE-RADISH

Scrape or mince the horse-radish. Mix with a little salt, a teaspoonful of vinegar, a teaspoonful of sugar, and a tablespoonful of cream. *Good with cold beef or mutton.*

144

SAUCE — LIMES OR LEMMETJIES (D)

Take 50 limes, cut a cross at one end, but not deeply enough to separate them into pieces. Put on them ½ lb. of salt in a deep jar or bowl, pour on them 6 bottles good colourless vinegar, let them stand for a month, stirring them occasionally with a wooden spoon. When settled, bottle the clear liquor, and the thick liquor when filtered ; the limes can be used for flavouring soups, pie-meat, or any savoury dish. The best vinegar for the above is acetic acid, which makes common-strength vinegar by mixing one part to 6 parts of water.

SAUCE — MAYONNAISE
(Mrs. Becker's, German)

The yolk of 1 hard-boiled egg mashed very fine, add to it the yolks of 2 raw eggs and 2 tablespoonfuls of best Lucca oil, added drop by drop, stirring constantly one way until quite thick; to this add 2 table-spoonfuls vinegar, some pepper, salt, mustard, and a little pinch of sugar and cayenne.

SAUCE — MAYONNAISE
(Mrs. Jackson's)

Ingredients:

3 eggs (yolks only)	½ tsp. of salt
3 tbsps. oil—Lucca	½ tsp. sugar
3 tbsps. ordinary vinegar	Some cayenne
1 tbsp. tarragon vinegar	2 sps. Yorkshire relish
½ tsp. white pepper	4 tbsps. cream

Put the yolks with pepper, salt, etc., in a round-bottomed basin; stir with a wooden spoon, adding first salad oil, then vinegar, cream, etc., until all looks like thick cream. Will keep if closely corked.

SAUCE — ONION, FOR SHOULDER OF MUTTON

Peel four or five white onions, put them in salt and water for half an hour; then boil in a saucepan, well covered with water, till soft; drain thoroughly; chop fine; mix with melted butter, according to the previous recipe for melted butter. *This is a most delicious sauce for boiled leg or shoulder of mutton.* See Sauce (Butter, melted).

SAUCE — OYSTER

About one and a half dozen oysters, raw or potted, to a half pint of good white sauce; a seasoning of cayenne pepper. Cream used instead of milk in the white sauce is a great improvement.

SAUCE — PARSLEY

Two spoonfuls of chopped parsley added to melted butter or white sauce.

SAUCE — PIQUANTE
(INDIAN)

Ingredients:

8 oz. green mangoes or apricots	4 oz. onions
8 oz. raisins	2 oz. garlic
8 oz. salt	8 oz. ginger
8 oz. sugar	½ a bottle of lime juice
4 oz. red chillies	3 bottles of vinegar

Pound the several ingredients well, add the vinegar and lime juice; close the jar well, and for one month expose to the sun; shake and stir it well *every day*. Afterwards strain into bottles. The residuum is excellent chutney.

SAUCE FOR PUDDINGS
(BESSIE'S)

Ingredients:

½ a cup of clear brown sugar	½ a cup of sherry (or a wineglass of
½ a cup of water	brandy)
Dessertsp. maizena	

Stir maizena and sugar in half a cup of water till it is smooth, and let it boil; then add the wine or brandy. Time, ten minutes. This will do for any boiled pudding. *Cheap.*

SAUCE — TOMATO, TO USE SAME DAY

Boil one dozen tomatoes to a pulp; strain through a soup strainer, add salt, pepper and cayenne. Very nice with chops or cutlets, adding an ounce of butter, a teaspoonful of sugar.

SAUCE — TOMATO, TO KEEP
(MRS. DAN CLOETE'S)

Ingredients:

40 large ripe tomatoes	2½ bottles of vinegar
¼ lb. coarse salt	2 tbsps. of ginger
2 tbsps. of sugar	2 tbsps. of coriander seeds
2 tbsps. of cloves	6 large onions; a little garlic may
2 tbsps. of mace	be added
3 horse-radish roots	8 large red chillies or more

Take forty very ripe tomatoes cut into quarters, sprinkle with a quarter of a pound of salt, let it stand for three or four hours; drain off the water. Put the tomatoes in a stew-pan with all the spices tied in a muslin bag, slightly bruised. Boil for at least three hours, then strain through a coarse sieve; boil again for half an hour, bottle whilst hot.

SAUCE — TOMATO
(A VERY GOOD RECIPE)

Ingredients:

40 lb. ripe tomatoes	2 oz. black pepper
1 oz. peeled garlic	2 oz. cloves
2 lb. loaf sugar	4 oz. ginger
1 lb. salt	3 quarts of the best vinegar
1 oz. cayenne, or 8 red chillies	

First boil and strain the tomatoes until the skins and seeds separate freely, strain through a coarse sieve that will retain seeds and skins. To this juice add the above ingredients tied in a muslin bag. Boil all well for an hour or more, till the juice is quite creamy and thick. Bottle and cork securely; keep in a cool place.

SAUCE — TOMATO
(MRS. JACKSON'S)

Take eight pounds of tomatoes, cut up and stew till tender. Take eight large onions, two cloves of garlic, the rind of six lemons, six bottles of vinegar, one spoonful of cloves, one spoonful of allspice three tablespoonfuls of ginger, three tablespoonfuls of salt (spice to be crushed and put in a bag), fourteen red chillies; boil all well together for four hours, strain through a sieve. Add the juice of six lemons. Cork while hot.

SAUCE — TOMATO (D)
(MISS FOSTER'S, HANDED DOWN FROM HER GRANDMOTHER)

Take 8 pounds of tomatoes, wipe them and cut them up and sprinkle half a pound of kitchen salt over them. Next day boil in an enamelled saucepan, adding eight large onions, sliced, one garlic, eighteen red chillies, two ounces of ginger, just cracked, one tablespoonful of mixed allspice and mace, four bottles of vinegar—a bottle holds two and a half breakfast-cups. Boil all till quite soft, then strain through a colander and boil again a few minutes. Lastly, bottle and cork. This sauce will keep a year.

SAUCE — FOR VEGETABLES, BOILED (D)
(MY OWN)

Rub a dessertspoonful of butter and one of fine flour well together. Add two spoonfuls of boiling water or milk, a little salt; and when stirred quite smoothly over the fire for a few minutes, add a tablespoonful of cream. Good with boiled beans.

147

SAUCE — WHITE, FOR HOT BOILED CHICKEN (D)
(MRS. ETHERIDGE'S)

Ingredients:

2 tbsps. of flour	A little salt
1 oz. butter	A little white pepper
1 pint of milk	Some button mushrooms
A little lemon-peel	

Stir flour and butter together; boil the milk, add to the flour, and stir till creamy; add the juice of the boiled chicken. The chicken to be previously boiled in a floured cloth for one and a half hours.

SAUCE — ANOTHER WHITE
(MRS. D. CLOETE'S)

Ingredients:

1 dessertsp. of maizena, or corn-flour	A little salt
1 oz. of butter	A little white pepper

Stir the flour and butter well together dry (this prevents the sauce becoming lumpy); pour over it half a teacupful of *boiling* water; stir on the stove till thick, then remove; add the yolk of an egg and juice of a lemon well beaten up, and pour over chicken.

SAUSAGES
(OUR OWN)

Ingredients:

12 lb. of minced meat	$\frac{1}{2}$ tsp. of allspice
8 lb. of fat (fresh bacon)	$\frac{1}{2}$ tbsp. of mace
2 oz. of pepper	$\frac{1}{2}$ tbsp. of thyme and sage, dried and
3 tbsps. of salt	pounded
$\frac{1}{2}$ tbsp. of grated nutmeg	1 pint of claret

Take the lean part of one or two legs of mutton, and any scraps that fall away in cutting up a pig. Mince all this, taking care not to let any sinew come with it, then mince the fat; mix all ingredients well together. Have ready some nicely cleaned skins, and stuff the mince into them with a sausage-machine. Will keep for eight or ten days. When wanted, grill on the grid-iron or in a pan; time for grilling, a quarter of an hour. This quantity makes a great deal; half would do for a small party.

SAVOURIES.—*See* Bloater Toast, Cheese-straws, Eggs (Italian), Savoury Toast, Pudding (Cheese), and Soufflé (Cheese).

SAVOURY — ANCHOVY TOAST (D)
(MRS. BLAIR'S)

Beat well two yolks of fresh eggs. Add one tablespoonful of anchovy sauce, one dessertspoonful of Worcestershire sauce, and a little red pepper. Beat all well together and put into a saucepan, with a piece of butter the size of a walnut, and put on the fire. Keep stirring till it is boiling, and spread on buttered, hot toast fingers. Serve very hot.

SAVOURY — CHEESE (D)
(Miss Adeane's)

Ingredients:

1 oz. butter	1 gill water
2 oz. of flour	2 oz. grated Parmesan cheese
2 small eggs	

Put the butter in a stew-pan with the water and season with pepper and salt. Boil and add the flour—stir this over the fire for four minutes, then mix in the Parmesan cheese and the eggs. Mix all well together.

To fry this mixture have a pan of good clear fat boiling; place in it a wire frying basket, then press in some of the cheese mixture through a colander into the fat and fry a golden brown. It must be served very hot.

SAVOURY — PENGUIN EGG (D)

Mash hard-boiled penguin eggs very fine, add a little bit of butter, some anchovy paste, a little cayenne and salt, and spread on hot buttered toast.

SAVOURY — SARDINE (D)

Bone the sardines, and halve. Fry in a small omelette pan with a mixture of the oil in the tin, cayenne, and anchovy sauce. Or bake in a hot oven and serve on toast *hot*.

SAVOURY MIXTURE — TO POUR OVER MEAT

Melt an ounce or more of butter in a stewpan; mix in a tablespoon of made mustard, a little black and cayenne pepper, and a tablespoonful of stock; beat well. This is good to pour over a grilled chop or steak.

SAVOURY SPREAD — GREEN BUTTER (D)

Ingredients:

2 oz. parsley, with cut stalks	4 oz. butter
3 oz. anchovies, or paste	

Boil the parsley till tender, then press out the juice from it. Wash, boil and pound the anchovies fine, or use anchovy paste; mix with the parsley thoroughly into 4 oz. fresh butter and pass through a fine sieve. Press into the shape of a cream-cheese and keep in the cool till required.

SAVOURY TOAST

Ingredients:

4 boned sardines	4 oz. of butter
1 tsp. of Worcestershire sauce	½ saltsp. of cayenne

Pound the ingredients with the sardines, and spread on hot buttered toast.

SCONES — FOR FIVE O'CLOCK TEA

Ingredients:

2 lb. of flour   4 oz. of butter or fat
1 pint of milk   1 tsp. of baking-powder

Mix all well together; roll out half an inch thick, and cut with a wineglass. Bake twenty minutes. Cut in two, butter, and send in hot.

SCONES

Ingredients:

1 lb. of flour   A few currants, if liked
2 oz. of butter   ½ lb. of sugar
1 tsp. of baking-powder   1 egg

Beat the egg in half a cupful of water; mix *quickly and thoroughly* with the other ingredients. Divide into rounds, which cut into four little cakes each and bake.

SCONES (D)

Ingredients:

½ lb. self-raising flour   ½ tbsp. sugar
2 oz. butter   Salt

Rub a little flour, salt and butter well together; then mix with a knife into half a cup of cold water, or milk. Beat well with a knife for a few minutes, and roll out and stamp into round shapes with a wineglass. Bake in a hot oven as for pastry. (The proper thing for baking scones is a " girdle," i.e., a round flat sheet of iron with a handle from side to side like a kettle's, to hang over an open fire.

SHAPE — COLD MEAT

Butter a plain mould; chop up any kind of cold meat you may have; add some stock, warmed with about three ounces of gelatine, flavoured with pepper, salt, nutmeg, and lemon-juice. Have some hard-boiled eggs cut in quarters, garnish the mould with them, pour the mixture into the mould. Turn out when cold.

SHEEP'S BRAINS (D)

First wash the brains in cold water, then pour boiling water over them to whiten them. Dip them in egg and bread-crumbs, seasoned with pepper and salt. Fry for a few minutes in boiling dripping or butter till they are light brown.

SHORTBREAD — ANOTHER

Ingredients:

1 lb. flour
¼ lb. sugar
½ lb. butter

A large handful of ground rice
Season with nutmeg

Mix the ingredients with flour, rub in the butter until it becomes a dough; roll out and cut into shape. Bake in a moderate oven.

SHORTBREAD — SCOTCH
(EMILY'S)

Ingredients:

1 lb. flour

9 oz. butter

Rub well together; roll out and cut. Put pieces of candied peel across each cake. Bake twenty minutes.

SHORTBREAD
(MRS. CLOETE'S)

Ingredients:

2 lb. flour
4 eggs

12 oz. sugar, finely powdered
1 lb. butter

Rub the flour and sugar well into the butter, make into a stiff paste with four eggs, roll to double the thickness of a penny. Bake in a warm oven for twenty minutes.

SOETKOEKIES.— *See* Tea Cakes.

SOETKRAKELING — SWEET CRACKNELS
(OLD DUTCH)

Ingredients:

1 lb. flour
1 lb. sugar
½ lb. butter

3 eggs
A tbsp. of cinnamon
A tsp. of potash

Mix, roll out and make in shapes like the figure 8, and bake on flat pans for twenty minutes.

SOUFFLÉ — CHEESE

Ingredients:

½ oz. butter
1 tbsp. flour
½ pint milk
Breakfast-cup of grated cheese

Yolks of 3 eggs
Whites beaten to a froth
A little salt and pepper—cayenne

Melt the butter, mix with the flour, add milk slowly, salt, and cayenne; then add grated cheese and yolks of eggs, lastly the whites of the eggs. Put into a flat buttered dish; leave to bake a nice brown. Serve hot. Time, twenty minutes.

SOUFFLÉ — ANOTHER CHEESE

Ingredients:

½ lb. cheese   Mustard
1 quart milk   Cayenne
3 eggs   Salt

Cut the cheese *very* thinly, mix with the eggs well whisked, then add about one eggspoonful mustard, a little cayenne and salt, a very little cold milk. Set the quart of milk to boil, add a teaspoonful of butter; pour on the cheese, etc. Bake a light brown. *Can be eaten hot or cold.*

SOUFFLÉ — EGG
(Miss Bonnie Cloete's)

Ingredients:

6 eggs   Juice and peel of a lemon
6 tbsps. sifted sugar   A little nutmeg

Beat the whites and yolks separately, add the yolks to the sugar, lemon-juice, and peel, and a little nutmeg, and lastly, *just before* putting in the oven, the *whites*, which must be a perfect froth. Mix all thoroughly, but lightly, and only just before you want it, *as it can't stand a minute,* or the yolks will sink. When baked it ought to be frothy brown sponge. Takes ten minutes. *Serve immediately.*

SOUFFLÉ — TAPIOCA

Ingredients:

1 tbsp. tapioca   1 pint of milk
2 oz. of white sugar   4 eggs

Soak the tapioca in water till quite soft, then set it to boil till it is the consistency of porridge, sweeten to taste; flavour with vanilla or lemon-peel. When cold whisk up the eggs separately, beat up with the pudding, pour into a soufflé mould. Bake twenty minutes, and serve *immediately.*

SOUP — BROWNING FOR

Put about four ounces of brown sugar, and half an ounce of butter, into a stewpan; set it on the fire to brown, stirring all the time with a wooden spoon that it may not burn. When sufficiently melted, stir in a pint of boiling water; let it boil, and skim well. When cold, bottle and cork. A tablespoonful or more will colour your soup.

SOUP OR STOCK — HOW TO CLARIFY

About three or four quarts stock boiled the previous day, well skimmed; whites of two eggs, well whisked, stirred into the stock; then put on the fire to boil. After it has boiled up once, draw it away from the fire; pour in a cup of cold water; let it stand for five minutes; strain through a fine cloth placed over a sieve; it will be clear and good. Stock for clear soups must be made strong, as it loses strength by being clarified.

SOUP — BROWN
(MY MOTHER'S)

Make a good stock of either neck of mutton (three pounds will make two quarts of excellent stock) or shin of beef. Add some fried onions; let all boil well together. When strained, add two spoonfuls of *brown* flour. Take a spoonful of sugar and a little butter; let them melt together till a dark brown. Mix with the flour a good glass of dark wine, eight cloves, a blade of mace, some pepper, bruised; add all to the soup; let it boil for two or three hours. Serve with toasted bread, cut like dice, and fried in butter.

SOUP — CUCUMBER OR MARROW (D)

Peel a large cucumber and lay it in cold water for half an hour. Throw away the water. Cut the cucumber into pieces about an inch thick and put the pieces, reserving a few, in a saucepan with salt, pepper, an onion, a sprig of parsley, and about 2 quarts of good stock, either of veal, mutton, or an old fowl. Simmer till the cucumber is tender, and then strain through a colander or sieve. Fry, *without browning*, 1 oz. of butter and 1 oz. flour, and pour on this some of the cucumber purée. Mix all together, stirring till it boils, then add some milk to make the soup the right consistency. Just before serving add the yolk of an egg, a little lemon-juice, and a spoonful of cream. Cut the reserved cucumber pieces into dice, and put in the soup, after boiling them till tender. Marrow may be used the same way.

SOUP — CURRY
(CAPE)

Head and feet of sheep, lamb, or calf, boiled till quite tender in three or four quarts of water. The next day, when cold, remove all the fat. Cut the meat small, and take out all the bones; brown an onion in fat; add two tablespoonfuls of curry-powder, one tablespoonful of flour, a teaspoonful of brown sugar, two teaspoonfuls of vinegar or lemon. Stir all together in the liquid in which the meat, etc., has boiled. Serve in soup tureen, with boiled rice handed round separately on a plate. *A homely dish.*

SOUP — HARE
(HOME RECIPE)

Ingredients:

Remains of cold roast hare	2 oz. brown flour
Some good stock	1 tbsp. brown sugar
1 doz. cloves	½ pint of port wine
½ oz. whole black pepper	2 small onions, fried

Trim off the best parts of the cold hare and put on one side. Chop all the bones, etc., and simmer for an hour in a few quarts of stock flavoured with the above seasoning. Strain through a sieve on the pieces of cold hare; let it boil once. Serve with toasted bread or very small square fried sippets.

SOUP — LIMPET OR PERIWINKLE (D)
(MRS. CLOETE OF ALPHEN'S)

Collect half a bucketful from the rocks below low tide mark in the winter months, their season. Put them in fresh water to kill them and rid of sand. Scrape the shells clean, pound them in a mortar, put in a pot, cover with water and boil. When done, strain through a coarse linen cloth, and add good beef or mutton stock to it in the proportion of one cup to every three cups of periwinkle broth. A couple of onions have been boiled in the meat stock. One dozen peppercorns, same of allspice, one tablespoonful of flour, and one of burnt sugar is added to the mixed stocks. Lastly it is poured into a tureen into which a good tumbler of wine has been put, and served with sippets of toast.

People at the seaside might like to try this nourishing soup.

SOUP — MULLIGATAWNY

Ingredients:

1 fowl (it may be an old one)	1 oz. of tamarinds, drawn in a cup
2 oz. of curry-powder	of hot water
1 dessertsp. of Indian curry-paste	1 tsp. or more of salt
2 onions	1 dessertsp. of chutney
1 tbsp. of butter or fat	1 tbsp. of flour
1 tbsp. of brown sugar	

Cut the fowl into small pieces, as for chicken curry. If an old one, let it boil gently for four or five hours, with two or three quarts of water. If you have a neck of mutton, or any other meat that will make some stock, you may add a little to this. The next day remove the fat and strain the soup, putting back any nice pieces of fowl. A few slices of ham may also be added to make a good stock. Brown the onions, mix all the ingredients, add to the soup, and let it boil for a couple of hours. Send in hot, with boiled rice on a separate dish.

SOUP — OX-TAIL

Ingredients:

2 ox-tails	5 cloves
¼ lb. of lean ham	1 tsp. of peppercorns
1 head of celery	1 bay leaf
2 carrots	1 wineglassful of ketchup
2 turnips	1 wineglassful of port wine
2 onions	3 quarts of water
1 bunch of savoury herbs	

Cut up the ox-tails, separating the joints; put them in a stewing pan with an ounce and a half of butter, one head of celery, two onions, two turnips, two carrots, cut in slices, a quarter of a pound of lean ham, cut very thin, the peppercorns, savoury herbs, and one pint of water; stir over a quick fire for a short time, to extract the flavour of the herbs, until the pan is covered with glaze; then pour in three quarts of water; skim it well, and simmer slowly for four hours, until the meat is tender. Take it out, strain the soup, stir in a little browned flour to thicken, add port wine, ketchup, and head of celery (previously boiled) cut fine; put the tails back into the stew-pan of strained soup; boil it up for a few minutes and serve. This soup can be served clear by omitting the flour, and adding to it carrots and turnips cut in fancy shapes. These may be boiled in a little soup, and put into the tureen before sending to table.

SOUP — PALESTINE, FROM JERUSALEM ARTICHOKES (D)
(Miss le Sueur's)

Wash and pare the artichokes and put them in a stew-pan with a small lump of butter, 2 strips of bacon, 2 bay leaves. Let them steam or simmer for 10 minutes, pour on cold water to cover the artichokes, then boil till soft and pass through a kitchen strainer and sieve. Add enough milk to the liquor to make it like gruel. Heat and when ready to serve, add a few spoonfuls of cream. Instead of adding water, mutton or veal, or other white stock, may be used.

SOUP — PALESTINE, ANOTHER (D)
(Miss le Sueur's)

Instead of boiling the artichokes in cold water, use stock from the knuckle end of a leg of mutton, or of veal, or any white meat, and when boiled and strained add a teacupful of milk as you would for potato soup.

SOUP — PIGEON, FOR INVALIDS

Ingredients:

1 pigeon	2 quarts cold water
¼ lb. veal	

Boil this down to a good broth very slowly till reduced to less than half, strain and let it get cold, remove all the fat. Boil it up when required, and thicken with a little sago, or a teaspoon of maizena rubbed in butter; add salt and pepper to taste.

SOUP — POTATO

Ingredients:

2 quarts of white stock	Some white pepper
6 large mealy potatoes	A little cayenne
1 oz. of butter, rolled in a tbsp. of	Salt to taste
flour	½ teacupful of cream
1 onion	

Put two quarts of white stock into a stew-pan; take six large mealy potatoes, boil and mash them till they are sufficiently soft to pulp through a sieve, with an onion boiled tender; add to the stock. Thicken with butter rolled in flour, and season with pepper, salt and cayenne; just before serving stir in the cream, and *do not boil again.*

SOUP À LA REINE
(MY OWN)

Ingredients:

2 quarts of nice white stock (may	Some nutmeg
be boiled from an old fowl)	White pepper
1 cup of fine bread-crumbs	A large cup of good cream
1 onion	

Put an old fowl in a stew-pan with enough water to cover it well; let it simmer for three or four hours; if the water has diminished, add a little more, *hot.* About a pound of neck of mutton or veal may be added, and an onion. Let it boil till you have a good stock, skim well; let it cool, and strain. The next day, when it has boiled up, add the nutmeg, bread-crumbs, pepper, and salt, and, just before serving, the cup of cream. Can be served with toasted bread cut in dice.

SOUP — TOMATO
(MY OWN)

Take about a dozen nice ripe tomatoes, boil quite tender, with an onion; mash, and strain. Add to two quarts of good stock; thicken with a pat of butter tossed in flour; flavour with a green chilli, cut up, just before serving.

SOUP — TORTOISE

I know of several instances where children seemed to be just *wasting away* at the ages of two and three, and have been strengthened and restored by a soup made by boiling down the whole tortoise, after chopping off its head, scrubbing it well, and then boiling it well till the parts separate. *The juice strained and taken.* To kill a tortoise, our old cook, Abraham, used to scratch its back, and when the tortoise put out its head he chopped it off.

The legs of the tortoise after it is boiled, and the liver (which is a special delicacy), after the removal of the gall-bag, eaten with lemon and pepper and salt, is much appreciated by invalids when they can take nothing else (of course it is an acquired taste). It is also very nice when scalloped with a little butter and bread-crumbs.

STEAK — PICKLED

Lay two pounds of steak in a dish with sliced onions, half a dozen cloves, two dozen whole peppers, a bay leaf, sprig of thyme, marjoram and parsley, a tablespoonful of salad oil, enough tarragon vinegar just to come up to the steak; let it soak for twelve hours, turning occasionally. Then take it out, and grill the steak in a hot pan, turning constantly. Stew the mixture, add a teaspoonful of salt, and let the steak simmer in it, taking out the spices, etc., before serving in a hot dish. *Enough for six people.*

STEAKS FROM THE UNDERCUT OF BEEF (D)
(Mrs. Becker's)

Take two lb. of undercut, or rump steak, wash it in warm water quickly, cut two inches thick, and chop well with a blunt knife, this process makes it very tender; lay it in a pie-dish and pour some milk over it, leaving it to soak for an hour.

Now take some onions, cut in rings, and fry them in fat a light brown. Keep these hot. Put half an ounce of butter in the frying-pan and heat it well. Roll the beefsteaks in a mixture of flour, fine bread-crumbs, pepper and salt, and fry them in the hot pan on a quick fire, turning constantly. Be very careful not to put a fork in the steaks, or all the richness will ooze out, but turn them with a knife. When brown, which will take about 8 minutes, pop the steaks on a hot dish, heap the fried onions on top of the steaks, and serve quickly. *Very good.*

STUFFING FOR DUCK, TURKEY AND GOOSE

Duck.—Boil the gizzards and liver till tender, and chop them up very finely, mixing with them bread-crumbs, sage, onion, pepper, salt and a little butter.

Turkey.—Bread-crumbs, butter, nutmeg, pepper, salt and thyme. Chestnut stuffing is also very good, or a stuffing of sausage-meat.

Goose.—Half a dozen potatoes boiled and mashed; add butter, sliced onion, pepper, and salt.

SWARTSUUR
(A homely Cape Dish)

Ingredients:

3 lb. of ribs of mutton	12 peppercorns, finely bruised
1 onion	½ tbsp. of brown sugar
2 oz. of tamarinds	Salt
6 cloves	

Cut meat as you would for curry, put in a stew-pan with the onion and a pint of water. When it has simmered for an hour, take out a cup of the boiling stock, skimming the top so as to remove all the fatty particles. Stir into the boiling soup a large cup of fine flour;

stir well over the fire till it is a thick dough, now set to cool. When *quite cold* work into the dough one or two eggs; of this make dumplings the size of a *walnut*.

After the cup of soup has been taken from the meat, stir into it the tamarinds soaked in a pint of boiling water, spices, etc.; let it boil well, and half an hour before serving stir in the dumplings. *Serve as an entrée.* The old recipe had the blood of a duck instead of tamarinds.

SWEETS.—*See* Butter-scotch, Cocoanut, Tameletjies, and Apples, Blancmange, Cake (Tipsy), Charlotte Russe, Cheesecakes, Chipolata, Creams, Custard, Deliciosa, Dick's Dish, Jellies, Meringues, Omelette (sweet), Pancakes, Puddings, Soufflé (Egg and Tapioca), Salads (Fruit), Tarts, Tartlets.

SWEETS — BURNT ALMONDS (D)

Boil one pound of sugar in one cup of water till it sugars, put in a pinch of Armenian bohl to give it that rich reddy-brown colour, and some powdered cinnamon. Dip the almonds in this mixture.

SYLLABUB
(MRS. ETHERIDGE'S)

Ingredients:

½ pint of white wine	2 oz. loaf sugar
1 pint of rich cream	Juice and peel of a small lemon

Rub the sugar on the peel to extract all the flavour from the peel, then add to the cream, and whisk well. Take about one ounce of sifted sugar and add it the last thing, as it tends to make the cream thicker. Put into glasses. *Excellent.*

For another Syllabub Recipe, *see* Trifle.

SYRUP — LEMON
(OLD CAPE)

Squeeze the juice of fifty lemons, and for every quart of lemon juice take three pounds of sugar. Let the lemons and sugar dissolve in an earthen jar placed in a saucepan of boiling water. Let it simmer in this manner till all the sugar is melted and the whole a rich, thick syrup. Bottle when cold, and cork well. The lemon-juice to be strained before mixing with the sugar. *A delicious drink in hot weather.*

SYRUP — ANOTHER LEMON
(G. VERSFELD'S)

Ingredients:

6 lb. of sugar, and 4 bottles of water, boiled to a syrup, and strained	1 oz. tartaric acid dissolved in a tumbler of water
¼ tsp. of oil of lemon	

Stir all together; let it settle, then bottle and cork. A little taken with soda water, or plain water, is very refreshing in summer.

T

TAMELETJIES
(A FAVOURITE CAPE SWEET)

For two basins of sugar take one of water, boil into a syrup. Clarify with an egg, boil briskly till it is all frothy; then fill little square paper shapes or ramaquin cases with this, after having mixed with it some almonds and grated lemon-peel, or nartjie (Tangerine orange) peel. Let it cool before serving.

TAPIOCA.—*See* Rice Milk.

TART — APPLE
(FROM AN OLD GERMAN COOKERY BOOK)

Ingredients:

Puff paste	¼ lb. butter
Apples	4 eggs
Almonds	1 cup sugar
1 pint milk	Pounded cinnamon

Line a tin dish with puff paste, peel and quarter one dozen apples lay them in the dish, also some blanched and pounded almonds, half a bottle of milk, butter beaten to a cream, four eggs, and one cup of sugar and some cinnamon to taste, all mixed together, poured into the dish covering the apples. Bake in an oven for an hour or more. I have found that anything requiring some time to bake must be covered with a tin plate at first, which can be removed when half-done.

TART — COCOANUT, KLAPPERTERT
(FROM A VERY OLD DUTCH BOOK)

Rasp two cocoanuts into their weight in sugar, add a good spoonful of butter, a cup of milk; and some cinnamon. Boil all together till it is quite stiff; then line a tart-dish with puff paste, and pour the mixture in. Bake for half an hour. *Very good.*

TART — COCOANUT ANOTHER WAY
(OLD DUTCH)

Grate the cocoanut very fine, take the weight in sugar, half an ounce of butter, one egg, white and yolk whisked separately, some cinnamon. Mix well together; line a tart-dish (ordinary tin plate) with puff paste. Bake in a quick oven till a nice brown.

Another way is to boil the cocoanut in a syrup made from the sugar and when cold, add the egg and butter; but the first has been tried and is *very good.*

TART — GERMAN (D)
(Mrs. Smith's from Graaff-Reinet)

Line an open tart-tin with Crust for beefsteak or German tart (see recipe), fill with jam, and bake on the floor of the oven for an hour. Treacle can be used and covered with a lattice or stars of pastry laid over it.

TARTS — ICED FRUIT (D)
(Mrs. Earle's)

Make the crust of fruit tarts separately—and place them when cold over the pie-dish, to which it is fixed with raw white of egg. In baking, the shape of the crust is kept by filling the pie-dish with clean crumpled kitchen paper. The fruit is previously stewed and allowed to get cold, or in the case of soft fruit like strawberries, the fruit is only cooked by pouring boiling syrup over it. Iced strawberries, with the space between fruit and crust filled with cream, whipped and iced, is almost as much a surprise " when the pie was opened " as the " four-and-twenty blackbirds! "

TART — MILK
(Old Dutch Specialité)

Ingredients:

1 pint of milk	A tbsp. of maizena
2 tbsps. of sugar	2 eggs
A tbsp. butter	A stick of cinnamon

Boil the milk with sugar and cinnamon, stir butter and maizena and a little cold milk together, pour into boiling milk. Boil for five minutes, pour into a basin, and when cold add two eggs well whisked. Line a tart-dish with paste, pour in this mixture, and bake for twenty minutes.

TART — ORANGE (D)

The oranges are divided into segments, and all the white taken off. A good short crust has been made and baked beforehand. A boiling hot syrup is poured over the oranges (they are not otherwise cooked), and the crust then put on when the oranges are cold, with white of egg, as in the recipe for Iced Fruit Tarts.

TART — DUTCH POTATO, AARTAPPELTERT
(Mrs. Myburgh's, from an old Dutch Recipe Book)

Ingredients:

1 lb. potatoes	10 sweet almonds
½ lb. loaf sugar	25 bitter almonds
8 eggs	Some rose-water

Boil the potatoes well, mash *very* fine; beat the yolks and whites separately; mix the yolks with the sugar; then add potatoes, then the whites, and lastly almonds, blanched and pounded with rose-water. Weigh the potatoes before you peel and boil them. Bake as you would a sponge-cake in a moderate oven for an hour.

TART — ANOTHER POTATO

Ingredients:

1 lb. potatoes (weighed before peeling)	20 bitter almonds
	½ lb. sugar
180 sweet almonds	8 eggs

Mix like the other. Line a tart-dish with puff paste and fill with this mixture. Bake a nice brown.

TART — POTATO
(A SIMILAR CAPE RECIPE, MRS. MYBURGH'S)

Ingredients:

¼ lb. potatoes (boiled and mashed)	6 well-beaten eggs
¼ lb. sugar	100 sweet almonds
Rose-water	25 bitter almonds

Blanch and pound the almonds with rose-water, mix with the sugar; stir in the potatoes. Bake in a pie-dish lined with puff paste.

TART — WALNUT
(AN OLD GERMAN CAKE. MRS. VAN DER RIET'S)

Ingredients:

A stale sponge-cake	2 eggs
100 walnuts	1 sp. of sugar
1 pint of milk	

Take a hundred walnuts (or a grated cocoanut); shell and pound the nuts—there should be a teacupful. Make a custard of the milk and eggs, and a spoonful of sugar. Add the pounded walnuts, stirring until it thickens, then pour into a basin to cool. Cut your cake into slices (a plain round mould is best), putting them together carefully; then put the bottom piece on a dish, cover it with some of the walnut custard, put the slice so as to fit, and put on some custard, and so on till the cake is built up again. Of the whites of the eggs make an icing. Ice the whole cake; ornament the top with pieces of walnut and some little bits of icing coloured with cochineal. If cocoanut is used instead of walnut, boil it with sugar into a syrup, as you do cocoanut ice. *An excellent way of using up a stale sponge-cake.*

TARTLETS — MARMALADE CREAM

Line some patty-pans with puff paste; now fill them with this mixture—one tablespoonful of apricot marmalade, the yolks of two eggs, one white, the weight of one egg in butter and in sugar. Whip all to a cream; put into the little tins. *To be eaten cold.*

TASSAL

(AN OLD-FASHIONED UP-COUNTRY WAY OF CURING MEAT IN THE OPEN AIR, POPULAR WITH TRAVELLERS)

Take any meat, beef, venison, springbok, etc. Cut the meat in long strips about three inches thick, sprinkle slightly with salt, pepper, a little coriander seed (bruised), and vinegar; leave for a day, then hand to dry; if wanted, just soak a little and grill on the coals.

The Boers and travellers find it most nourishing in travelling, when fresh meat cannot be procured.

TEA — TO MAKE GOOD

Be very careful to rinse the teapot with boiling water. Allow a teaspoon of tea for each person and one for the tea-pot, pour *boiling* water into the pot, let it stand for five or six minutes. Then pour it off into your silver teapot, and keep hot with a cosy by the fire for late-comers.

On no account keep the tea standing on the leaves for more than ten minutes. The Dutch people often improve their tea by collecting orange-blossoms in the season, and keeping them with their tea in the caddy.

TEA BISCUITS — EXCELLENT
(MRS. BECKER'S)

Ingredients:

1 lb. crystallized sugar	1 tsp. of pounded rock ammonia, or
1 lb. flour	baking powder
½ lb. butter	1 tsp. of vanilla essence
3 eggs	

Beat the butter to a cream with the sugar, then add the whites and vanilla; mix the ammonia dry with the flour, then mix all well together, like dough for bread; roll between the hands pieces of the dough, and cut with a knife to the size of a pigeon's egg. Bake in a quick oven for fifteen minutes.

TEA BISCUITS — BRAWN

Put a handful of flour on a board and mix with half a teacupful of cream. Roll out thin and cut with tumbler or wineglass. Bake in a very hot oven for a few minutes.

TEA BISCUITS — BUTTER

Ingredients:

3 lb. of flour	½ lb. of butter
1 lb. of sugar	5 eggs
2 tbsps. of pounded rock ammonia or sal volatile, or baking-powder	2 tbsps. of caraway seeds, slightly bruised
	1 tumbler of cold water

Whisk up the eggs and mix with butter and sugar; then mix all ingredients together. Knead well, roll out with rolling-pin, prick with a fork, and make into shapes with a wineglass, or any other mould. Bake for half an hour on buttered tins.

TEA BISCUITS — COCOANUT (D)
(MISS VAN RENEN'S)

Ingredients:

6 oz. sugar	½ lb. desiccated cocoanut
The yolk of an egg	The whites of 4 eggs

Mix well and shape in small pyramids. Bake in a moderate oven.

TEA BISCUITS — COOKIES
(MRS. FLEMING'S BOOK)

Mix together one pound of white sugar, one pound of flour, and half a teaspoonful of carbonate of soda; rub into a quarter of a pound of butter. Make into a soft paste with three eggs, well beaten, and a dessertspoonful of cream or milk; essence of almonds to taste. Roll out half an inch thick, cut with a wineglass. Bake ten minutes in a moderate oven.

TEA BISCUITS — LEMON (D)

Ingredients:

1 lb. flour	2 lemons
1 lb. sugar	2 eggs
½ lb. butter	

Heat the flour slightly, then rub the butter into it, mix in the sugar and the grated peel of the lemons. Beat the eggs well and add to the juice of the lemon. Stir the whole together and knead well; roll out the paste thin, cut into shapes and bake to a light brown.

TEA BISCUITS — VIENNA (D)
(MRS. DRUMMOND HAY'S)

A pinch of salt, one ounce of castor sugar, and 2 ounces of butter are rubbed into a quarter of a pound of flour; you then beat up the yolk of an egg and a tablespoonful of milk together, and add to the flour. Roll out this paste very thinly and stamp it out in rounds, half with a smaller round from the centre ; bake all on a buttered paper on tins in a moderate oven a quarter of an hour.

Now chop up or grate 2 or 3 ounces plain chocolate, put it in a saucepan with two tablespoonfuls of water and let it boil four or five minutes, then stir in four or five ounces icing sugar. Let it just come to the boil, and spread quickly on the biscuits—the whole ones—and then press on them those which have the centres cut out, filling up the cavity in the centre with crystallized cherries, or other candied konfyt, or with cream whipped very stiffly. For a children's party, hundreds and thousands could be sprinkled over the cream.

TEA CAKES — LITTLE CHOCOLATE (D)
(MRS. DRUMMOND HAY'S)

Beat six ounces of butter to a cream, add the same weight of fine white sugar and two well-beaten eggs, half a pound of white flour, a quarter of grated chocolate and a pinch of baking-powder, mix all together well with some vanilla flavouring. Butter about a dozen little tins and pour in the mixture. Bake in a quick oven and turn them out carefully, when done, on a sieve to cool.

TEA CAKES — CHOCOLATE CAKES (D)
(MISS MAY VAN RENEN'S)

Beat half a pound of butter to a cream, add a quarter pound of fine white sugar, three well-beaten eggs, a quarter pound of grated chocolate, three ounces of fine white flour, two ounces blanched and pounded almonds, about a saltspoon of baking-powder. Butter your little tins and line with buttered paper. Pour a little of the mixture into each tin, bake in a quick oven. Turn them out when the reed or straw you stick in to see if it is done comes out dry, and when cold, ice them with vanilla icing.

TEA CAKES — LITTLE DROP (D)

Ingredients:

¼ lb. butter	1 oz. almonds, blanched and
3 eggs	pounded
¼ lb. sugar	20 drops vanilla essence
3 oz. flour	

Beat the butter to a cream, add the sugar next, and then the yolks of eggs. Beat all well together. Now add the flour and the other ingredients, keeping to the last the whites of eggs well whisked. Drop little drops of the mixture on buttered paper and bake in a slow oven.

TEA CAKES — GERMAN (D)
(MISS BECKER'S)

Ingredients:

6 oz. fine sugar	1 lb. flour
1 egg	Vanilla or lemon flavouring
¾ lb. butter, stirred to a cream	

Stir all well together and roll out thinly. Cut out into fancy shapes or with a small round tin. Egg over and strew with sugar mixed with pounded almonds.

TEA CAKES — GERMAN (D)
(MISS BECKER'S)

Ingredients:

1 lb. of butter
1 lb. of sugar
9 eggs
1 lb. of flour
50 almonds

¼ lb. of currants
1 tsp. of cinnamon
½ tsp. of rock ammonia, or baking-
    powder

Stir the butter to a cream; mix well with fine white sugar, the yolks of nine eggs and whites of two; beat with sugar and butter; then add one pound of flour and half a teaspoonful of finely powdered rock ammonia. Butter some paper, and put into pans in a quick oven; drop the mixture with a spoon on the paper, and sprinkle over the top cut up almonds, mixed with currants, cinnamon, and crystallized sugar. *Most delicious little cakes.*

TEA CAKES — HILDA'S

Ingredients:

1 lb. of flour
1 lb. sugar
4 eggs
¼ lb. butter
1 doz. cloves, pounded

A tsp. of sifted cinnamon
A tsp. of soda
A tsp. of cream of tartar
25 almonds

Beat up the yolks and whites well. Mix with the butter and sugar and the almonds pounded; mix all well with the hand, and put on buttered pans, about the size of a walnut, with the point of a knife. Bake for twenty minutes.

TEA CAKES — JUMBLES (D)
(WEST INDIAN, BROUGHT FROM JAMAICA BY MRS. MONIER WILLIAMS)

Ingredients:

8 oz. butter
1 egg
6 oz. finely powdered loaf sugar

12 oz. flour (4 of which to be self-
    raising)

The sugar and butter to be well rubbed with the egg, and the flour added by degrees. When well mixed, take pieces the size of a walnut, roll them into pencil shape, about five inches long, keeping them well rounded. Coil them round flat on the baking-dish, round and round, but keeping the coil flat and closely curled. When baked it is a very pretty and dainty tea cake.

TEA CAKES — RICE

Ingredients:

1 tea-cup of ground rice
2 eggs

Essence of vanilla or almonds
1 tea-cup of sifted sugar

Whisk up the sugar and eggs in a round basin well; then add rice, whisk for twenty minutes; add an eggspoonful of essence; put a teaspoonful in patty tins; bake in a quick oven from five to ten minutes.

L

TEA CAKES — ROCK CAKES
(MISS LILLA SPENCE'S)

Ingredients:

¼ lb. butter
1 lb. flour
¾ lb. moist sugar
2 eggs
¼ lb. currants

¼ a tumbler of brandy (or white wine)
Some lemon-peel
50 pounded almonds

Whisk butter with the sugar, then yolks, and whites of eggs. Mix all the other ingredients with the flour; knead into the eggs and butter; lastly, mix the brandy or wine; drop on buttered paper in tins, and bake for half an hour.

TEA CAKES — ROCK CAKES (D)

Mix half a pound of flour with a quarter of sugar. Rub in a quarter of butter; moisten with an egg beaten with two tablespoonfuls of milk. Add some currants; put on a buttered tin pieces the size of a walnut; bake in a quick oven.

TEA CAKES — ROUT (D)

Ingredients:

2 lb. flour
1 lb. currants
1 lb. sugar
1 lb. butter

2 eggs
A tbsp. each of orange-flower water, sweet wine and brandy

Mix all together. Drop in spoonfuls on buttered paper and bake in a hot oven.

TEA CAKES — SPONGE

Ingredients:

6 eggs
¼ lb. of flour
¾ lb. sugar

The grated rind of a Lemon or nartjie

Whisk the yolks well with the sugar till bubbles rise, whisk the whites stiffly; then add flour and peel. Bake in little tins, well buttered, in a moderate oven for half an hour.

CAKE — TEA OR BREAKFAST, WELSH TITIENS (D)

Ingredients:

3 grated apples
¼ lb. mixed butter and lard
1 good tsp. of baking-powder

½ lb. flour
2½ tsps. brown sugar

Rub all together in a bowl, stir up with a fork, and add a few currants. If you have no apples, add a few spoonfuls of milk. Sprinkle a little flour over when well stirred and knead on a board. Then roll out with a rolling-pin, cut in circles and lay on a girdle greased with a little buttered paper. When one side is done, turn over, and then sprinkle the brown top with sugar (the sugar side must not be turned down or it will stick). They must come to table very hot. Some people omit currants.

TEA CAKES — SOETKOEKIES
(VERY OLD DUTCH RECIPE. MRS. VAN DER RIET'S)

Ingredients:

4 lb. of flour	4 eggs
3 lb. of good clear brown sugar	1 tbsp. of potash of carbonate of
1 lb. butter	soda
½ lb. of sheep-tail fat	2 tbsps. of cloves, finely pounded
1 lb. of pounded almonds, or 200	2 tbsps. of cinnamon
almonds pounded without	A tumbler of dark wine (claret)
blanching	

First rub flour, sugar, butter, spices, and soda well together; lastly, add the wine; knead all well together. If potash is used, it must be dissolved in the wine—is best mixed overnight. Roll the dough out with a rolling-pin; make into shapes with a wineglass or any thin shape. Bake on buttered tins. The old Dutch people put a small piece of citron preserve in the centre of each little cake. Bake for twenty minutes in a tolerably brisk oven. *Very good.*

TEA CAKES.— *See also* Oblietjies, Scones and Cakes.

TOAD-IN-THE-HOLE
(AN ECONOMICAL DISH FOR A LARGE FAMILY)

Ingredients:

2 lb. loin of mutton	1 oz. melted suet or clarified drip-
An eggspoon of pepper	ping
A dust of nutmeg	Half a tsp. of carbonate of soda,
A tbsp. of tomato sauce	stirred into the dry flour
1 pint milk (skim), or buttermilk	Batter made of 1½ cups of flour

Cut the mutton in cutlet shapes, roll in flour, salt and spices; lay them in a dish, and pour over them the spoonful of tomato sauce, and a quarter of a cup of water. Mix up the batter, and pour on the top. Put the pie-dish in the oven. Takes one and a half hours to bake.

TOFFEE — COCOANUT

Ingredients:

1 cocoanut	1 lb. sugar

Grate a *fresh* cocoanut ; boil the sugar with the milk of the cocoanut and a cup of water; when nice and thick, add the grated cocoanut. Stir all the time, till you see it coming off quite clear from the sides, then take off. Grease the dish on which you pour it, mark it out with a knife in squares, and let it get cold. *Very good.*

TOMATO BREDIE
(CAPE)

Cut up two pounds of ribs of mutton and an onion; stew in a flat pot for an hour. Cut up and add eight or ten tomatoes in slices, also a teaspoonful of salt, a pinch of sugar, and half a red chilli. If there is a great deal of liquid, remove the lid, and let it simmer till it is all a rich creamy-looking sauce. Remove the fat. Serve with plain boiled rice. *A very nice entrée.* See Bredie.

TOMATO STUFFED

Extract some of the inside of the tomato; mix bread-crumbs, cheese, chopped onion, and pepper, with an egg. Stuff the tomato with this mixture; sprinkle over with bread-crumbs and a piece of butter. Bake for an hour. Tomatoes plainly cut in halves and sprinkled with crumbs and butter, and fried, or baked in the oven, make a very nice vegetable.

TRIFLE
(MRS. ETHERIDGE'S BOOK)

Ingredients:

1 tumbler of madeira or sherry	$\frac{1}{2}$ lb. of macaroons
2 wineglasses of French brandy	1 pint of rich boiled custard
4 sponge biscuits	1 pint of syllabub

Soak four sponge biscuits and half a pound of macaroons in the Madeira and French brandy. Then cover the bottom of a glass dish with half of these, pour over them a pint of rich custard previously made, then lay the remainder of the soaked biscuits on them, and pile over the whole to the depth of two or three inches the whipped syllabub, well drained; the whipped syllabub to be made the day before, or some hours before, as follows: Take half a pint of cream, half a glass of light wine, and a dessertspoonful of sifted sugar; take a clean, dry whisk, and whip the cream to a stiff froth with the wine, adding the sugar last of all. When the wine has drained to the bottom, carefully skim the light frothy cream, and pack it on the top of the last layer of macaroons. *Excellent.*

TROTTERS — STEWED (D)

Prepare and boil some trotters as for brawn, and in the same way; when quite tender remove the bones and fat. Then stew the trotters with a few slices of onion. The onion may be slightly browned in fat, or it may be put in just as it is, with pepper, a small piece of mace, a dash of grated nutmeg, and thickened with some finely grated bread-crumbs. (Any pieces of stale white bread, dried in a cool oven and pounded, are most useful for thickening soups, or rolling cutlets or fish in for frying—far nicer than fresh crumbs. They should be kept ready, tightly corked in glass bottles.) To the stewed trotters add, just before serving, the juice of a lemon, whisked up with the yolk of an egg. This dish makes a nice entrée, and is inexpensive—half a dozen trotters costing 6d.

TROTTERS IN BATTER (D)

When you are stewing trotters for brawn, reserve some of the pieces of meat, without the jelly. Dust a little pepper, salt, and nutmeg over each piece. Have ready, meantime, a nice batter. Dip the pieces of meat in this and fry. It is a nice dish for breakfast, or as an entrée. Very delicate invalids may eat it and will enjoy it.

TROTTERS — CURRIED (D)

To trotters which have been cleaned, cooked, and had the bones removed, add 1 tablespoonful Cartwright's curry-powder, a large sliced, browned onion, a tablespoonful vinegar, and a dessertspoonful very brown sugar. Boil, and serve with rice and apple chutney. (*See* Mrs. Jackson's recipe for this.)

TURKEY — BOILED

Hen turkeys are preferable for boiling, on account of their whiteness and tenderness. They should not be dressed until they have been hung two or three days, as they will not be tender. Pluck the bird carefully, and singe with a piece of paper; wash well, and wipe with a dry cloth; cut off head and neck; draw the strings or sinews of the thighs; cut off the legs at the first joints, draw the legs into the body, and fill the breast with forcemeat, or stuffing; run skewers through the wings and middle joint of leg quite into wing and leg on opposite side; break the breastbone, and make the bird look as round as possible.

Way of cooking. Put the turkey into sufficient *hot* water to cover it, let it come to the boil, then carefully remove all scum; if this is attended to there is no occasion to boil the bird in a floured cloth, but it should be well covered with water. Let it simmer very gently for one and a quarter to one and three-quarter hours, according to the size, and serve with either white, celery, oyster, or mushroom sauce, a little of which should be poured over the turkey. Boiled ham, bacon, tongue, or sausages should accompany this dish; and when oyster sauce is served, the turkey is always stuffed with oyster forcemeat.

A simple stuffing for turkey. Soak a penny loaf of stale bread in either milk or water, press well; take a good lump of butter or suet, a little sugar, pepper, nutmeg, salt, some sweet herbs, an egg. Mix all well together, and stuff turkey or fowl.

V

VAN DER HUM.—*See* Liqueur.

VEAL CAKE

Ingredients:

3 lb. veal	Salt, pepper, cayenne
½ lb. pork	A few cloves, pounded
¼ lb. of bread-crumbs	

Mix all well together with a couple of raw eggs, put into a plain mould, steam for two hours, then put into an oven to dry a little; turn out when cold. Cut in slices. A nice luncheon dish.

Mutton done the same way is very good to eat hot.

VEAL — ROAST FILLET OF

For an 8 lb. fillet, take out the bone and fill up with the following stuffing: ¼ lb. of suet, ½ lb. of bread-crumbs soaked in milk, a few sweet herbs, a little nutmeg, pepper, and an egg or two mix all well together. Skewer up the joint in a round form (larding it with nice fresh bacon is a great improvement); cover the veal with a buttered paper; let it roast very gently; baste it well with some butter or fat. About half an hour before serving, pour over the joint half a tumbler of wine, with a teaspoonful of flour mixed in it, which makes a nice rich gravy. (Takes three hours in·an oven.)

VENISON
(MY OWN)

The Duiker is considered very good, and also the Springbok, which, however, is very rare in the Western Province of South Africa.

The forequarter is generally used for " Buck soup "; the saddle (cut like a saddle of mutton) being the best joint for roasting, and must hang for six or seven days. After the outer skin is taken off, there still remains a thin white fleece, which *must* be taken off before larding the venison. Take a firm piece of fat bacon cut into equal strips, and proceed to lard either with a larded needle or a pointed knife. Venison is much nicer roasted in a flat *Dutch baking-pot*, with a good piece of butter and a spoonful of good lard or fat. Put the joint on with a little water. If a saddle, turn it upper side down at first, and an hour afterwards put some wood-coal on the cover of the pot. Having basted the joint well, roast it a nice brown, and half an hour before serving pour over it a tumbler of dark wine and a little vinegar, with a dessert-spoonful of flour mixed in. Stir the gravy well. This gives a nice glaze to the meat and imparts a very good flavour. If done in the oven, cover the joint with a buttered paper and baste frequently.

The Steenbok and the Grysbok are very plentiful in some districts and are very good to eat too.

VEGETABLE MARROW STUFFED — ENTRÉE
(MRS. D. CLOETE'S)

Ingredients:

3 lb. veal	A few sweet herbs
½ lb. ham or good bacon	2 oz. butter
2 eggs	2 oz. bread-crumbs
Pepper, salt, parsley	

Mince veal and ham together, pound to a paste in a mortar slightly rubbed with garlic, pass through a coarse sieve; put back into the mortar, work into the paste the butter, bread-crumbs, spices, the yolks of one or two eggs, and the flavouring. Cut average-sized vegetable marrows (the pretty, small-shaped ones) into halves, scoop out the seeds, etc., fill with the above mixture. Wrap up each marrow in a piece of buttered paper tied with a string, lay them all closely together in a buttered dish, cover this with a tin plate, and put in the oven. When you think they are done, remove the paper carefully, lay them in a dish, and serve with a nicely-flavoured gravy made with a little stock, thickened with the yolk of an egg, and a glass of wine or a little lemon mixed just before serving.

VEGETABLE MARROW AS AN IMITATION OF APPLES
(CAPE, OUR OWN)

Take a large vegetable marrow—the white kind, with lumps all over the outside—cut it in thin slices, after having peeled and taken out the soft pulp and seeds. Proceed to slice it very thinly. Butter an enamelled pot; put layers of this vegetable marrow, and sugar (for one good-sized marrow take a large breakfast-cup of sugar), a tablespoonful of flour or bread-crumbs, ten cloves, a tumbler of wine and vinegar mixed—pour the wine over the last layer of vegetable marrow and sugar—also a pinch of salt. Let the stewpan simmer for two hours, stirring carefully for fear of burning. Very good with roast duck or goose.

VEGETABLES — SAVOURY

Take a young heart-shaped cabbage, parboil, and lay it on a dish and cut it in half, carefully remove the inside, stuff the cavity with nicely-flavoured mince, or a preparation as for Frikkadel (*see* that recipe); put the two halves together, and tie with a piece of tape and a thin skewer, put it into a saucepan with a little stock, and a few pieces of bacon; let it simmer for an hour or more. *Serve nice and hot.* A slice of toast or some crumb of bread in a muslin bag, placed in the water in which cabbage is boiled or stewed, absorbs the peculiar cabbage smell out of the water which is so disagreeable, and the muslin bag can be thrown away when the vegetable is dished.

W

WAFELS
(Mrs. Breda's, old Dutch)

Ingredients:

¾ lb. butter	A tbsp. sifted cinnamon
1 lb. flour	½ pint wine
½ lb. sugar	8 eggs

Beat the butter to a cream, add sugar; mix alternately one egg and one spoonful of flour with the butter and sugar, then add cinnamon and wine. Grease the iron and warm; put in the dough and close, turning the iron first on one side and then on the other while baking. Serve with sugar and cinnamon.

WENTELJEFIES

Take twelve slices of thinly cut stale white bread, butter well, soak in milk (not too much), then whisk up eight eggs, lay the bread in the egg, then fry in hot lard or fat, as you would fritters. Serve with sugar and cinnamon. *This is an old Dutch dish.*

Y

YEAST — FOR MAKING HOME-MADE BREAD
(Our Own)

Take two quarts of boiling water, an ounce of salt, three cups of meal. Put the salt into a saucepan, pour on it the *boiling* water, strew on it gradually three cups of meal, then cover closely, putting a cloth between the lid and pot to absorb the steam. Set it overnight in the warmest corner of your stove. At six o'clock next morning stir into it a cup of boiling water; stand the saucepan on some hot ashes, and soon it will begin to ferment. When ready for use it will have a frothy appearance and a disagreeable odour. Pour it into six pounds of meal, mix with warm water, and knead into bread.

YEAST — RAISIN (D)

Crush in a mortar half a cupful of raisins, and put in a two-pound fruit bottle, with one tablespoon of sugar; fill the bottle to within two inches from the top with tepid water.

It will be fit for use when the raisins *all float on the surface*. This quantity is sufficient for 4 lb. of meal. Mix and knead the dough over-night, use all the liquid, pouring it on the bowl and adding warm water to the yeast sufficient to mix into the ordinary consistency. Start at once making fresh yeast by putting in the same quantity of raisins, but *don't wash the bottle*, and leave a few old raisins in it. This sets it fermenting next time.

YORKSHIRE PUDDING.— *See* Puddings.

INDEX

174

175

Also of interest . . .

**POPULAR NORTHERN SOTHO
DICTIONARY:
SOTHO-ENGLISH/ENGLISH-SOTHO**
T.J. Kriel
335 pages 4 3/8 x 5 3/8 $14.95pb
0-7818-0392-6 (64)

**VENDA DICTIONARY:
VENDA-ENGLISH**
N.J. Van Warmelo
490 pages 6 x 8 1/2 $39.95hc
0-7818-0393-4 (62)

**FULANI-ENGLISH
PRACTICAL DICTIONARY**
F.W. Taylor
264 pages 5 x 7 1/2 $14.95pb
0-7818-0404-3 (38)

**HAUSA-ENGLISH/ENGLISH-HAUSA
CONCISE DICTIONARY**
Nicholas Awde
250 pages 4 x 6 $14.95pb 0-7818-0426-4

**LINGALA DICTIONARY AND
PHRASEBOOK
LINGALA-ENGLISH/ ENGLISH-
LINGALA**
Thomas Antwi-Akowuah
120 pages 3 3/4 x 7 $16.95pb
0-7818-0456-6 (296)

**UNDERSTANDING EVERYDAY
SESOTHO**
98 PAGES 5 1/4 X 8 1/2 $16.95pb
0-7818-0305-5 (333)

TWI BASIC COURSE
225 pages 6 1/2 x 8 1/2 $16.95pb
0-7818-0394-2 (65)

Hippocrene Travel Guides
for Africa

(NEW) GUIDE TO SOUTHERN AFRICA
Botswana, Lesotho, Namibia, South Africa, Swaziland, Zambia and Zimbabwe (revised edition)

This guide to the great game reserves, cities and beach resorts of Southern Africa has been completely revised and supplemented with much additional material. It is packed with essential advice on where to go and what to see and includes many photos and maps of the region.

From the Kruger National Park in South Africa to the Etosha Pan in Namibia, from Botswana's Okavango and the Kalahari to Victoria Falls in Zimbabwe, the rapids of the Zambesi and the Luangwa Valley in Zambia, this guide covers all the legendary wildlife areas, as well as the museums, shops, sporting events and other points of interest in urban areas like Cape Town, Johannesburg and Blomfontein.

300 pages, 5 1/2 x 7 1/2, 0-7818-0388-8 $19.95pb

NAMBIA: THE INDEPENDENT TRAVELER'S GUIDE
By Lucinda and Scott Bradshaw

"A comprehensive guide ... covering all the practical details of travel in Namibia for the adventurous budget or luxury traveler." *—Book News*

This guide provides information on food, lodging and sightseeing in all four of the distinctive regions that compromise the country: the Namib Desert, the Great Escarpment, the Northern Plains and the lowlands in the East, as well as the new national parks in Mudumu and Mamili.

313 pages, 5 1/2 x 8 1/2, 0-7818-0254-7 $16.95pb

KENYA AND NORTHERN TANZANIA
by Richard Cox

"An invaluable book for tourists and Kenya residents alike"*—Sunday Nation*

This guide is a "must" for anyone contemplating a visit to the area. The general information explores all the opportunities available to travelers. Historical backgrounds of given areas, advice on how to drive and get around the back roads of Kenya and Tanzania as well as national park maps provide the information to plan and budget a trip.

200 pages, 4 x 7, 0-87052-609-X $14.95pb

INTERNATIONAL LITERATURE

TREASURY OF ARABIC LOVE:
POETRY QUOTATIONS AND PROVERBS IN ARABIC AND ENGLISH
Edited by Farid Bitar

A treasury of Arabic love poetry that spans the centuries pre-dating Islam through the twentieth century. Poets include: Adonis, Gibran Kahlil Gibran, Saïd 'Aql, and Fadwä Tûqän. This bilingual edition features both English and the original Arabic script.

128 pages 5 x 7 0-7818-0395-0 $11.95hc (71)

THE WEATHER IN AFRICA: THREE NOVELLAS
Martha Gelhorn

"This is a surprisingly good book" —*New York Times*

The look and feel of Africa, the scents and colors are so true that one might be there, and the weather is perfect. Europeans live in this magnificent scenery but their inner weather, very different from the sunshine around them, is turbulent and predictable.

263 pages 5 1/2 x 8 1/2 0-9087-101-1 $14.95pb (443)

MOROCCO THAT WAS
Walter Harris

"Many interesting sidelights on the customs and characters of the Moors ...intimate knowledge of the courts, its language and customs ...thorough understanding of the Moorish character." —*New York Times*

338 pages 5 1/2 x 8 1/2 0-90787-1402 $14.95 (446)

(All prices subject to change.)

TO PURCHASE HIPPOCRENE BOOKS contact your local bookstore, or write to: HIPPOCRENE BOOKS, 171 Madison Avenue, New York, NY 10016. Please enclose check or money order, adding $5.00 shipping (UPS) for the first book and $.50 for each additional book.